I Know You By Heart

by
Peter Broadhurst O.S.M.

Published by
CR Print, Dungannon
in Association with Servite Publications

Copyright © Servite Publications

First Published January 2009

First Edition

ISBN 978-0-9560683-1-6

Note from the Editor

Prior to sending out what is called "Letter One", Peter sent out a very brief note to his friends informing them that he had developed an asbestos related cancer known as mesothelioma. He also informed them in the letter that the prognosis was poor and that he had been given between six to twelve months to live with an absolute maximum of eighteen months. In the end Peter lived for almost three years and it was during this time that he wrote the letters published in this book. He wrote the letters for as long as he felt able to do so but increases in medication and physical debility eventually robbed him of the energy and mental clarity the task required. None of the letters have been edited or changed in any way since the time of writing and are offered in the hope that they might be of help to others.

EDITOR

Forward:-

This little book has its origin in a collection of letters that I wrote to friends after hearing that I had a terminal condition known as mesothelioma. Mesothelioma is a cancer that is caused by exposure to asbestos and during the course of reading the letters herein you will find out a great deal about the condition and the injustice that is perpetrated upon those of us who have been unfortunate enough to contract it.

This book has come about as a result of numerous people suggesting to me that the letters I had written to friends after hearing that I had developed this condition ought to be collated and placed into a book. Underlying this suggestion is the belief that the collection might be of help to others, particularly those with terminal conditions and those looking after them. Initially I was opposed to doing this for a variety of reasons that I won't go into at present. However, as time has gone on, I have dared to believe that the letters might not only be of interest to people but possibly help them on their journey and it was this thought that led me to agree to their publication.

The last fifteen to twenty years of my life has been devoted to the practice and teaching of contemplative prayer. The discipline of my way of life has brought to me many benefits not least of which has been an increasing ability to live from within myself and take seriously my own life experience. I suppose this could be called a reflective way of living. As well as this I have also learned to discern a sacramentality in the warp and weft of ordinary everyday life; how God leaves a trace of himself in all things and events.

This realisation has come about not through effort of will but the simple practice of being open to "what is" in a none judgemental way. Reality is always our friend, no matter how it may sometimes tear the very fabric of our being asunder at certain periods of our lives. For these difficult and possibly traumatic life situations to give us their blessing all that is required of us is to suspend our judgement. In other words, refrain from immediately labelling things as "good" or "bad", when in reality it would be more true to describe them as "pleasant" or "unpleasant". Such a change of perception is not easy for any of us but it is possible to "hold" a situation without immediately rushing to judgment.

This change of mind and heart is, I believe, the "metanoia" that is called for in the Gospels and it requires us to let go of our tendency to judge things and situations according to our own very limited perceptions. St. Paul tells us that, "We know that all things work together for good for those who love God, who are called according to his purpose (Rom 8:28).

In all of the letters contained herein I have tried to use my life experience in a positive way. This I have done not as an exercise in positive thinking but out of the conviction that there is something good to be found even in situations that afflict us. Such a concept has been a means of opening the inner doors of my life and living and I publish these letters in the hope that they encourage you to abandon the ground on which you are accustomed to stand and view life from a new perspective.

A constant source of support in my practice of prayer has been a little book whose simplicity belays its depth – "The Cloud of Unknowing". One of the major teachings of the Cloud is that whilst something of God can be known via the intellect the only real way of knowing God is to know him by Heart – hence the title for this little book.

In its pages of the Cloud and its companion volume, The Book of Privy Counselling I always manage to find something of worth. Something to validate my own perceptions, encourage me in my practice of prayer as well as challenge me to open up new vistas of perception. In my present illness I found the following words in the sister volume of the "Cloud of Unknowing", "The Book of Privy Counselling".

"Take the good gracious God just as he is, as plain as a common poultice, and lay him to your sick self, just as you are. Or, if I may put it another way, lift up your sick self, just as you are, and let your desire reach out to touch the good gracious God, just as he is, for to touch him is eternal health. The woman in the Gospel testifies to this when she says: 'If I but touch the hem of his garment I shall be healed.' She was healed physically; but even more shall you be healed of your spiritual illness by this lofty, sublime work in which your desire reaches out to touch the very being of God, loved in himself.

Step up bravely, then, and take this medicine. Lift up your sick self, just as you are, to the gracious God, just as he is. Leave behind all inquiry and profound speculation into your being or his. Forget all these qualities and everything about them, whether they be pure or defiled, natural or grace-given, divine or human. Nothing matters now except that you willingly offer to God that blind awareness of your naked being in joyful love, so that grace can bind you and make you spiritually one with the precious being of God, simply as he is in himself" (Bk Priv Counselling Ch2).

In these simple and rustic words the author writes of the balm that all of us need to cure us of our tendency to try and live our lives at arms length from God. Ill health, as I have experienced it, is a way of calling us "Home" and bringing about in us a different and more healthy way of being.

It was many years ago that I first read the words of St. John Cassian, "Experience is the teacher". They are words I have always clung fast to, for in them I recognise the Truth contained in the words. May this little book I have compiled enable you to value more deeply your own experience of life especially if you like me are fast reaching the point where your own death looms large. The past two years of my life have been both the best of times and the worst of times. It has been a time of great growth and fecundity but also a time of pain and loss. I think that St Paul expresses this well when he says:-

[2 Cor 4:16-18] "So we do not lose heart. Even though our outer nature is wasting away, our inner nature is being renewed day by day. For this slight momentary affliction is preparing us for an eternal weight of glory beyond all measure, because we look not at what can be seen but at what cannot be seen; for what can be seen is temporary, but what cannot be seen is eternal."

I am very conscious that this is a book whose ending I cannot write. I do not know either the time or date of my last letter and so I have to rely upon another to end this slim volume. I have asked Fr. Patrick Ryall O.S.M., the present Provincial of the Province of the Isles to make the last entry in this book which will be the homily he is to preach at my funeral mass. Patrick is a good and dear friend whose homily will provide a suitable end not only to this volume but as a testament to my life as Servite brother within The Province of the Isles.

My Dear Friends,

I am sorry that it has taken me so long to follow up from my last missive but as you will be aware the last few weeks have been phenomenally busy.

Since my last letter to you I have had a spell in hospital to remove the fluid from my chest wall. It is unfortunate that in the removal of the fluid air has got in and now I have what is called a pneumothorax. I had hoped to take a holiday in Rome soon after finishing my treatment at the hospital but the above condition prevents me from flying and the thoughts of travelling to Rome overland fills me with horror. I next see the chest consultant in a couple of weeks time and hope that the condition has righted itself in the interim. As far as I can see, my next course of treatment will be radiotherapy to the sites where doctors have made insertions into my chest wall to install drainage tubes or take biopsies. By so doing it is possible that they may have brought abnormal cells to the surface and the purpose of this very limited radiotherapy is to destroy any abnormal cells that have tracked through the wound to the surface.

As well as all these medical things I have also had to apply for state benefits. My efforts in this area have been greatly aided by an organisation called, Clydeside Action on Asbestos who have made sure that I obtain every financial advantage. They, together with the medical staff at Ninewells Hospital, have convinced me that I should take out a civil action against my former employers for compensation. Part of me feels somewhat guilty about so doing after spending years railing against "the compensation culture" but that is what I intend to do. A law firm in Glasgow will take on my case along with other cases against my former employers in the hope of obtaining some compensation. I would not undertake this action if I had any feeling of anger about what has happened nor would I do so if I personally were going to obtain financial benefit but it is my intention to donate whatever funds I manage to obtain to cancer charities. In this way I see myself as merely relocating funds from one source to another, making something "good" out of what feels to be a "bad" situation. My Order is in total agreement with my decision and is happy to relocate these funds as and when they come through. However, the firm that employed me has now been taken over by a multinational company and the company concerned is resisting payment of U.K. compensation claims against them. This means that it is likely that I will have journeyed to "the further shore" by the time matters are settled, however, my executors have the right to continue the claim in my name.

It is my intention to remain here in Tayport living independently for as long as I can. The house has two bedrooms and so it is possible for my sister to stay with me and she has expressed the desire to support me in what will be my final illness for as long as she is able to do so. For this and all the other wonderful kindnesses shown to me I am truly grateful. My sitting room is full of cards; so many that there are not sufficient surfaces to put them on! I treasure each one of them and feel overwhelmed by the love that has been shown to me. In many of the talks I have given I have often stated that the hardest thing for any of us to believe is that we are loved the way we are. That statement comes not from idle speculation upon a theme but from the world of experience and so I find myself at war within as I try to reconcile how I see myself with the outpouring of so much love and affection. What has been so wonderful in these communications has been the affirmation that I will be able to make this, the evening of my life, a positive experience for myself and others. Suffering without meaning or purpose would be cruel and too horrible to bear and so I constantly try to see where God is breaking though in what is happening. This is not a denial of reality but a refusal to label what is happening to me as either "good" or "bad". Most of you if not all of you will have been bored sometime and often by my recounting of the story of the old Chinese farmer with his "Good luck, bad luck, who knows?" Things are the way they are and it is we who have to accommodate ourselves to Reality. Again I have often quoted the great Jesuit spiritual director and writer Jean-Pierre de Caussade's definition of perfection, "accepting whatever comes from the hand of God at each moment of time". Well, I guess that I now have to move from a notional ascent to these words to the level of experience; another thing I have always spoken of!! I know that suffering and discomfort await me. It is this not death that frightens me but the process involved in my physical dissolution. However, when I have sought reassurance from the medical staff at the hospital they have assured me that my end will be as easy as it can be and they will do all they can do to help me die well.

Over the time remaining to me I will try to keep you up to date with what is happening in my now very limited world and share with you any reflections I might have. I realise that for some of you this might be too painful and open up issues that you are not ready to deal with at the moment. If you would rather not receive these "newsletters" please let me know and I will remove your name from this mailing list without any thought of there being a personal slight.

In the particular stage of life and living in which I now find myself relationships take on a different dimension. As I see it they now have an intensity that they did not have before. Perhaps that is due to the fact of there being so little time left to me and a desire not to waste what time there's left to me on trivia. A number of people have written or spoken to me saying how much they regretted not having spent time with me or not having gone to a talk I was giving. Such regrets are foolish for things are the way they are and it is pointless to indulge ourselves in regret. How much better to realise that the relationships we have on this earth are finite and let this discovery bring with it a resolve to live life with a new intensity and treasure each moment and each person rather than fill our lives with trivia.

I also find this "urgency" in nature too. In my garden I have a number of rose bushes coming into their second and last great "flush" of the season. Every time I look out of the kitchen window I find my eyes drawn to them because in my heart I know that it is unlikely that I will ever see so many blooms on the bushes again. I take time to simply look at things in a way I have seldom done before, rejoicing in simple presence. However, there is another side to such a realisation and this produces sadness because one realises that one is in the grip of a process that requires a continuous process of "letting go", a task that is not easy for any of us.

Yesterday I received notification from the Department of Work and Pensions that I have been awarded 100% disability with all the payments and "privileges" that go with that. Seeing this expressed in such stark terms upset me for a while and brought me face to face with the fact of my physical demise. Whilst one thinks that one has accepted this it is also important to recognise that death is too big to take in all at once. As I have said to numerous people, it's like eating an elephant - one can only take it in a spoonful at a time because it is much too big to swallow whole!

My hope is that, as I approach the end, my discomfort will not make me so self absorbed as to lose the sense of wonderment I now experience from time to time. How glad I am that my practice of meditation has, at least notionally, taught me the wisdom of "letting go". So much of the pain of my past life has been due to my clinging to things that I needed to let go of and, in the "holding on", creating my own misery!

Please keep me in your heart as I keep you in mine and I would also ask those of you in meditation groups to share with other members of your group this letter. So many kind people have written to me, too many to be able to respond to and this letter is an attempt to maintain the communion that we have been privileged to share one with another.

My Dear Friends,

I am delighted to say that on my last visit to the Respiratory Clinic I was told the good news that my pneumothorax has healed and so I am now able to fly. In my last letter I said that I was hoping to take a holiday in Rome. However, things have now moved on from there and I have decided against this plan. I find myself a little more breathless and tired than I was and the prospect of being a tourist feels as if it might be more of a challenge than a holiday. I will therefore "pass on" never having visited Rome but, in giving up the desire, I have accomplished something far greater. By not feeling the need to grab an experience but instead listen to the wisdom of my own body I have managed to reverse a customary way of behaving and achieved far more in life than a trip to Rome could have offered!

Rome will, therefore, be just one of the myriad of experiences that will be lacking in my life. All of us have "roads" we have never walked, experiences we have never had, dreams we have never lived out. Maturity demands that we realise that a lifetime is too short a period to live out all of our hopes and dreams and there comes a time when we need to be content for aspects of our life to be unlived, dreams unrealised. I have never been married and I do not know the intimacy and companionship that comes from such a relationship. However, this "lack" in my life has opened up for me so many other relationships that would have been impossible within the context of marriage. In a similar vein, I have never had a child of my own but in this deprivation I have had the opportunity to nurture the lives of so many others and watch as anxiously as any parent as they took their first faltering steps to independent life and faith-filled living. Things lacking or deficits in our lives can be situations that effect a positive result, as St Paul writes, " in everything God works for good".

I have had so many wonderful cards and letters, for which I am truly grateful, but one of them from Fr. Gerry Hughes, the author of "God of Surprises", made me laugh out loud when I read it. He wrote, "….and when you reach the next stage of your journey, may you not rest in peace, but continue sharing that freedom and peace with the rest of us!" I thought to myself, "Yes, that is how I would want it to be". I do not want to rest in peace but be an agent of love and freedom to people. What a wonderful thought it would be if one could become more effective in doing what one has attempted to do throughout the whole of ones life when one crosses to "the further shore".

I am glad to say that I am still fit enough to be able to walk Barclay my dog. Our walks are usually by the river because there are few hills! During these walks I see Dundee Law, a hill of several hundred feet in height, on the far bank of the river. I remember how, not too many years ago, I used to run up and jog down it four times as part of my training routine as a runner. I can see also the Sidlaw Hills, beyond Dundee, and remember the days when I would run out to the hills, run up them and over them before running back to Dundee. Memories of how fit I used to be come flooding into my mind as I see these hills: These memories of the past conflict with my present reality with its slow but relentless increase in

9

breathlessness. In this situation I realise that I have to let go of the image of how I was and learn to accommodate myself to a new unsought and painful reality.

I suppose that this happens to us all as we get older, in other words, what is happening to me is just an acceleration of an experience that is common to us all as we learn to be surrendered to "what is" with its attendant losses. I can't say that I find this process either easy or pleasant but I am convinced that my experience of meditation makes easier the task of "letting go", not just of the past, but letting go of all the things that can't be controlled. In meditation we awaken to the experience of "what is" by learning to sit in attentiveness to our word, which will spread from our practice into our ordinary life. It is in the emptiness of our heart that we discover our true essence which is unchanging amidst all the changes of life. Life is a gift that you offer back to God, and the gift that was a finite gift when it was given to us becomes, in the offering back, an infinite gift.

This November I will celebrate my fifty ninth birthday. I know that, baring a miracle, it will be the last occasion on which I will celebrate the gift of mortal life through my parents. I have received so much support from you my very dear friends that I thought it would be a delight if those of us who could might come together in silent prayer and simply be there in the "Being There" of God. I am going to be selfish here and suggest that everyone comes to me here in Tayport! We can gather at the Catholic Church in Tayport at 11-00am on Saturday the 6th of November (I promise that you won't freeze to death!). I would like to give a talk, we could then meditate and those who wish could come back to my house for a cup of tea and a snack. The address of the church is, Our Lady, Star of the Sea, Queen Street, Tayport. In order to provide sufficient snacks would you be kind enough to contact Margaret McBennett and give details of numbers coming. Her e-mail address is mm010c1302@blueyonder.co.uk and her 'phone number is 01382 778375. Don't worry that you have not had a response to your message – just come along! Perhaps those who live at a distance could offer a lift to others?

If you are unable to be present don't worry too much as I would hope to do this from time to time. The problem is not knowing how quickly my health will deteriorate and makes it impossible for me to undertake commitments, particularly those that involve travelling.

My Dear Friends,
            Two weeks ago I had a holiday in North Wales and on my way South called into a place called Hindley Green. Now I know for you this place name means nothing at all and why should it for it is a small, run down and insignificant spot between Wigan and the place of my birth, Leigh. However, for me it is a place that of late has been very much to the forefront of my mind for it was the location of a factory belonging to Turner Brothers Asbestos; a place I worked at from the 9th of October 1967 till 26th of June 1970. A short period of time but a time of momentous significance in my life for it was there that I was exposed to the asbestos fibres that will ultimately lead to my demise. The years I worked there were happy years for the company was considered to be one of the better employers in the area; providing as they did reasonably good working conditions and pay. When I think back to those times it is difficult to describe the feelings that I have about that period of my life. On one hand I remember the company as being a reasonably good employer and on the other hand it was where I was exposed to carcinogenic materials without adequate protection.

It was an attempt to resolve these ambivalent feelings that led me to visit the site of the factory and I thought that the holiday period following the factory visit would help ensure that I did not bring back to my home any "difficult" feelings. I was surprised at how anxious I felt as I travelled a well known and well travelled route, albeit over thirty years ago! Without any difficulty I located the factory, which is still in existence, and parked the car in the approach-way of the factory. It was a Sunday and the gates were locked and factory security men were in the "lodge" where they would have been at the time I worked there. The factory is now in multiple occupation; different companies occupying various parts of the site. However, the initials TBA, Turner Brothers Asbestos, are still proudly displayed upon the gates and surrounding railings and so it felt as if nothing has really changed over the years. The North and South Blocks of the factory still look the same, though the South Block, which housed the asbestos textiles and asbestos spray fibre divisions, did seem to have been modified. It was in the South Block of the factory that I was employed as a maintenance fitter some thirty five years ago.

Looking at the factory and remembering the hustle and bustle of former years induced a pricking of tears behind my eyes as I thought of the thousands people who must have passed through those factory gates. I realise that I can't be the only one who has been unfortunate enough to have developed mesothelioma. How many of us have there been and how many are there still who await a death sentence being pronounced over them as a consequence of going about their business within that factory. I found myself saying that there should be a memorial, other than the TBA initials on the gates and railings, to acknowledge that on this spot humanity made a terrible mistake.

Depending upon whom one believes: One might believe that the employers knew of the deadly consequences of the use of asbestos products. Alternatively, one can choose to believe that the employers were ignorant of the side effects of the material they were selling, seeing it as being a wonderful insulating and fireproof material. I do not know the answer to these questions but do know that a terrible mistake was made, be that mistake one of moral failure or a mistake made in ignorance.

How easy it is to put the past behind and forget those who have had to pay with their life for the grave mistake that was made. The company that I worked for has now been taken over by an American multinational called Federal Mogul who, because of claims for damage due to asbestos related diseases, has filed for Chapter 11 bankruptcy. This allows them to trade without making payments to those disabled by the very materials on which the company's wealth was founded. The difficulty experienced in trying to obtain benefits from the "polluter" is proof positive that the individual always fares poorly when faced with the "corporate". I believe this is illustrated quite well by this extract from John Steinbeck's "The Grapes of Wrath":-

"The owners of the land came onto the land, or more often a spokesman for the owners came... Some of the owners men were kind because they hated what they had to do, and some of them were angry because they hated to be cruel, and some of them were cold because they had long ago found that one could not be an owner unless one were cold. And all of them were caught in something larger than themselves.... If a bank or a finance company owned the land, the owner man said, the Bank - or the Company - needs - wants - insists - must have - as though the Bank or the Company were a monster, with thought and feeling, which had ensnared them. These last would take no responsibility for the banks or the companies because they were men and slaves, while the banks were machines and masters all at the same time... The owner men sat in the cars and explained. You know the land is poor. You've scrabbled at it long enough, God knows.

The squatting tenant men nodded and wondered and drew figures in the dust, and yes, they knew, God knows. If the dust only wouldn't fly. If the top would only stay on the soil, it might not be so bad...

Well, it's too late. And the owner men explained the workings and the thinkings of the monster that was stronger than they were... You see, a bank or a company... those creatures don't breath air, don't eat side meat. They breathe profits; they eat the interest on money. If they don't get it, they die the way you die without air, without side meat. It is a sad thing, but it is so. It is just so.. The bank - the monster has to have profits all the time. It can't wait. It'll die. No, taxes go on. When the monster stops growing, it dies. It can't stay one size...

We have to do it. We don't like to do it. But the monster is
sick. Something has happened to the monster...

Sure cried the tenant men, but it's our land. We measured it and
broke it up. We were born on it, and we got killed on it, died
on it. Even if it's no good, it's still ours...

We're sorry. It's not us. It's the monster. The bank isn't like
a man

Yes, but the bank is only made of men.

No, you are wrong there - quite wrong there. The bank is
something else than men. It happens that every man in a bank
hates what the bank does, and yet the bank does it. The bank is
something more than men, I tell you. It's the monster. Men made
it, but they can't control it."

It often happens that the institutions we have created tend to "have" us; they take over our
lives and we become slaves to "worldly spirituality" of the institution without us realizing
what has happened. This leads us to behave in ways that deny the truth of the mistakes we
have made, the damage we have done and the consequences of that damage to others; all
that matters is the survival of the company or institution.

Humankind needed someone to reveal how unfree we are and how we need to be saved
from ourselves and this was the mission of Jesus. He came to show us that we cannot live
well if we are alienated from our communion with the Divine or our relatedness to our
fellow human beings. It was a hard message for people to hear in the time of Jesus of
Nazareth and it is a hard message for us to hear today but hear it we must if we are to learn
to live in a humane and intelligent manner.

Next week I hope to spend a few days on the Isle of Iona with my Provincial, Fr. Patrick Ryall.
I will carry you there in my heart to this "thin" place, a place where the boundary between
heaven and earth is not so clearly delineated. Pray for me as I pray for you and may God
keep us all safe on our journey, both inner and outer.

My Dear Friends,

So much seems to have taken place since I last wrote to you. Soon after my last missive I developed shingles but I am happy to report that it had abated sufficiently to allow me to go to the Isle of Iona for a few days with Patrick Ryall my Provincial.

The light on Iona I have always thought to be very special, it has a quality that brings out the artist in us all as it plays with the hills, the stone of the Abbey and the Celtic crosses in front of the building. I have always considered that autumn and spring have a special light which is gentle and brings out the colour of things and the long shadows that it casts give items an almost mystical quality. As in all things, I am unsure if part of my perception is influenced by the knowledge that this may be the occasion of my last visit to this hallowed spot. Knowing this might possibly be the case makes my eyes "hungry" and creates the desire to take everything in before it is lost forever or, alternatively, perhaps it is a new found ability in me to see what "is"?

A special moment for me during my stay on the island was receiving the anointing of the sick during a mass at the Catholic House of Prayer. Mary Burn Murdoch, a lady well know to both Pat and myself, joined us for the mass and she like me received a sacramental anointing with oil. The chapel of the House of Prayer has a simple elegance. Behind the altar are long windows stretching from floor to ceiling. These windows, combined with the raised elevation of the house, enable one to see right across the Sound of Iona to the Isle of Mull. A repeated distraction when in the chapel was the appropriateness of this architectural feature: it is as if the architecture of the building is challenging one to take the sacred Presence from altar to the world beyond. This thought in turn brought to remembrance the words of a prayer from the Iona Community Worship Book, "..........Take us outside Lord, outside holiness, out to where soldiers curse and nations clash at the crossroads of the World. So shall this building continue to be justified. We ask it for your own name's sake."

A spirituality that takes one away from the human condition is, to say the least, suspect. One cannot move closer to God by moving away from people. Even if one is a hermit, one is a hermit for humanity otherwise it is a foolish and narcissistic way of life. The spiritual life should be a disciplined life that tones us up to meet new and undreamed of possibilities and challenges, things that formerly we felt incapable of either living or being. The only time when imagination should be suppressed is during times of meditation for our imagination needs to find links, symbols, meanings new directions and missions. If imagination is accompanied on its journey by intelligence and will, there will be focus and direction to our musings so we will not fall prey to delusion. Perhaps the greatest need in the world today is for clarity of perception. The world is full of people who would want us to share their prejudices and perceptions rather than see things as they are; for seeing things as they are often means seeing things in their complexity rather than taking in the "sound bites" to which we are accustomed.

The practice of contemplative prayer teaches us to see what actually is there and the deeper our practice the greater will be the clarity of our perception. The realisation that one does not see things as they are is the beginning of accurate perception. So much of what we see is conditioned by prejudice, hearsay and conditioning in its many forms and varieties. Only by breaking free from past conditioning can one see the beauty or horror of what is there; not what we think ought to be there but what actually is there!

To divide contemplation from prophesy is to damage and, possibly destroy both, for there is a unity between them. There are some schools of meditation that would seem to try and provide an escape from risk and struggle, purification of motivation and development of maturity. A true faith is a faith that is born of questioning and struggle before it becomes a certitude, any other form of faith is an ersatz faith. Contemplation has the desert as its birthplace, a place of struggle and purification. True prayer should never be seen as an escape from life and the common lot of mankind but as a sharing in the redemption of the world and of common life.

The god of much conventional religion is a being who lives beyond the world and although he may from time to time show an interest in what is going on in the world, generally he would rather not be disturbed. But the God of authentic Christian prayer is an involved and social God. The taking of humanity into the Godhead, which is what prayer is, embraces spirituality and politics, the inner and outer. True prayer is the movement of God to humankind and humankind to God, a rhythm of invitation and response. Many recent spiritual writers have described Western culture as suffering from a flawed consciousness insofar as there is a lack of an experience of transcendence. But the more we root ourselves in what is abiding the more compassion we have for our fellow men and women. The goal of prayer, grounded in the Incarnation, is the union of man with God. As St. Irenaeus (130-200AD) once wrote, "The Word became man in order to make us what he is himself". What Jesus achieved through Calvary was the union of mankind with God – it is this union which is the goal and climax of all Christian prayer.

As you may recall from my last letter I recently visited the factory where I worked thirty five years ago. Because of the emotions experienced at that time and the above thoughts I decided that I needed to try and aid the lot of those who like me are having their lives shortened as a result of contact with asbestos. Compared with diseases such as breast cancer, there is little in the way of public campaigning over the condition known as mesothelioma nor is there more than a fractional funding of research into it. Ken O'Byrne, former head of the British Mesothelioma Interest Group, who now works at St James's hospital, Dublin, is scathing about the lack of research money poured into the disease compared with say, breast cancer. "People think it will pass away. It has often been perceived as a disease of older working-class men and historically they tend not to get the best deal".

Mesothelioma is not the only asbestos related disease. Every year in the U.K. 4,500 people die from asbestos-related diseases and by 2020 it has been estimated that the substance will be responsible for over 10,000 deaths a year. In 1999 the U.K. joined many other countries in Europe to ban the importation, sale or new use of the last remaining form of asbestos allowed – white asbestos. The E.U. has banned asbestos as from 2005, and all the countries joining the E.U. from now on will be covered by that ban. However, the damage has already been done and we are now left with a legacy from the past that needs to be faced and dealt with.

The firm I used to work for, Turner Newall, has been taken over by an American multi-national, Federal Mogul, which recently went into Chapter 11 bankruptcy; a process that allows them to trade whilst defended from creditors. The company are trying to resolve their financial problems in a way that is unhelpful to British claimants such as myself. John Battle, Labour MP for Leeds West, is advising asbestos victims to ignore a direct appeal to them from asbestos company Federal Mogul.

Federal Mogul have paid for newspaper adverts and are writing to each victim to get them to support a company plan drawn up in their headquarters in the USA which cuts out the lengthy process of winding up asbestos company Turner & Newall. The plan proposes to set up a trust to compensate asbestos victims, but it will be based in America and already it is clear that under US law US claims by potential victims will take precedence over the claims of actual victims in Britain.

John Battle said, "Even the administrators, Kroll Buchler Phillips, have expressed surprise at this direct appeal that bypasses them and their attempts to salvage compensation for the British victims – such as those in Armley. My advice is that it's a waste of time responding to the American plan – we have to continue the fight with the administrators. Anyone who receives the voluminous documents sent with the plan should not respond."

I would not describe myself as a political person but there is a time when one has to espouse a cause and work for the betterment of ones fellow men and women. For ones prayer to be valid it must be rooted in true compassion for others, if this is not the case ones prayer is suspect. I like to think that my desire to make our world a more just place, a more compassionate place, has its roots in my prayer and meditation. I believe this to be the case because I find myself surprisingly energised by this cause though I realise that my purpose is simply that of being a catalyst. Without overtaxing myself I am seeing some of my local politicians with a view to encouraging them to develop an interest in the above issues and helping right the wrong that has been committed. This is a fight that I will not be able to see through to the end but one in which I hope to be able to motivate others by sharing with them a perception that I believe comes as a outcome of deep prayer and an understanding of the implications of "incarnation".

One of the high points of my year was the celebration of my birthday! The actual date of my birth is November the 9th but we anticipated the event here in Tayport on the 6th. Some ninety people turned up for the talk I gave and the silent prayer we shared had what the Society of Friends would describe as a "gathered" quality. Many thanks to all who came along and particular thanks to those valiant souls who prepared food and drink for all. One person asked me why I had not asked for five barley loves and two fishes. I said that last time I did this I ended up with twelve baskets of leftovers; happily this was not what happened on the sixth! (Alex Holmes wrote a piece on this gathering and I have attached his text onto this e-mail.)

I will be giving a talk on an Advent theme in Glasgow on Thursday the 9th in the Church of the Carmelite Monastery, 29, Mansionhouse Road, Glasgow G41. at 7-30pm. If you are free it would be good to see you but if you can't make the talk and would like to hear it, you can obtain a copy of the tape from Sr. Marie Helen, Carmelite Monastery, 29, Mansionhouse Road Glasgow G41 3DN. (Copies of the Tayport talk are also available from Marie Helen should you wish one.)

I will not be sending out any Christmas cards this year but please do not think that if you do not receive a card I do not think about you. Be sure that each of you will be held in my heart this Christmas and I pray that this year both you and I may come to share more fully in the divinity of him who came to share in our humanity.

My Dear Friends,

As I write I am very conscious of this being the beginning of a new year. As you will understand the past year for me has been, in the words of the opening chapter of Charles Dickens novel, "Tale of Two Cities", "the best of times and the worst of times" As you will also appreciate this is a situation that is likely to continue throughout 2005 as well.

A few weeks before Christmas I was spending a few days at our priory in the North of Ireland; Benburb. Whilst there I was walking in the grounds and came upon a tree whose branches were stark and bare: the leaves having dropped from the branches and formed an extensive carpet about the tree. I then noticed a host of aconites had forced their way through the fallen leaves and were thrusting their buttercup like flowers through the mat of deadness to the winter sun. I have always loved aconites and remember well how, when I lived at our Begbroke priory, I would eagerly await their coming. Each year they would force their way through the hard earth under the chestnut trees by the grotto to Our Lady and in doing so would be the first heralds of spring and fecundity.

But there in Ireland it seemed as if they, somewhat imprudently, had decided to poke their heads above the ground a month or more before their scheduled time. To me it felt as if this was a small miracle, an event of the greatest significance, and I found tears glistening in my eyes. Jung, the psychologist, wrote about what he described as "synchronicity" – moments when "outside" and "inside" things combine. That scene seemed to symbolise my life situation – how life, so frail and vulnerable, was breaking through deadness. I had just climbed the steep path from the river and so was very much aware of how illness is robbing me of the breath of life and yet within me I felt so very full of life. The feeling and the moment inevitably passed but the confirmation of an energised and affirmed mode of life remained.

Just before my trip to Ireland my oncologist told me that looking at my chest x-rays over the last months would seem to indicate that my cancer was progressing very slowly and, should the rate of growth remain the same, I may have another year of life in me. As you will appreciate, this news was quite the best Christmas present I have ever received. I have resolved to use the time that remains to simply live my life in the way I need to. I want to have time for my friends and say my prayers but also take up the cudgels for those afflicted with asbestos related diseases.

It was through the Macmillan nurses at the hospital that I discovered that there was a charity in the East of Scotland that supported victims of asbestos related diseases. Sadly local authorities do not support them in their work. They fail to provide them with office space and funding sufficient for them to have a welfare rights officer to help clients negotiate the labyrinth of benefit claims. When I needed to negotiate this maze I was helped by one of the two charities in the West of Scotland specialising in the care of asbestos victims. It was they who informed me about my financial entitlements and sent me the appropriate forms; made sure that the forms were correctly filled out; suggested a solicitor for my civil action against my former employers and offered me emotional support. I received wonderful help in negotiating the complexity of the social security system but the source of help was over a hundred miles from my home here in the East of Scotland. At present the charity in the East of Scotland working with people who have asbestos related diseases, Asbestos Action Tayside, is run by a small group of committed people from a private home in Kirkcaldy, Fife. As you will appreciate, there are limitations as to what a group that has no office and no funding can do to help those in need. Given their limitations they do a wonderful job but could do a better job with more resources and I hope to help them obtain those resources.

Not only have I been involving myself in this local issue but I have also been trying to obtain justice for those of us whose lives have been destroyed by a "magic mineral" that turned out to be a killer dust. It is a sad reflection upon our society that a company will spend millions on accountancy and legal fees as a way of avoiding paying compensation to those who suffer pain and death. I have been seeing and writing to members of parliament and members of the Scottish executive with the aim of establishing justice for asbestos victims. There is a generally held principle that "the polluter pays" in environmental issues but this does not seem to apply when it comes to human beings!

I believe that I have been very fortunate in having an extension to my life and I believe that such a "gift" has been given for a purpose. At the moment I am energised by the above causes but also realise that the time may well come when I find it too taxing or demanding. However, for the moment at least, I have the energy and I believe it to be a task laid upon me. I do not know if my aims will ever be achieved but I do know that I have to try and make the world a little more compassionate and just, before I leave it. To some it may seem that my actions are political but I would suggest that at root all problems are spiritual. As I get older the more convinced I become that this is the case. The purpose of religion is to put us back on Centre, to make us "concentric" rather than our present position of being "eccentric", off Centre. Only if everything is aligned upon That of God in us will our society and our world be compassionate and just.

When the disciples of John the Baptist, who was in prison at that time, came with a question for Jesus about whether or not he is the one to come he answers them by saying, "The blind see, the lame walk and the good news is preached to the poor". A spirituality that is too heavenly centred is of no earthly good to anyone! In Christ we see one who perfectly incarnates the compassion of God and shows us who we really are in our depths. In the incarnation, the unity of the human and the Divine, we see a pattern that is to be replicated in our lives. We are to be Christ today and that in turn suggests that all of us are involved in the creation of a more just and equitable world, a world united in the power of Love.

As I write I am aware of the feast of the Epiphany which has recently been celebrated or is about to be celebrated, depending upon where you live. This feast used to be one of the three great feasts of the Christian Church along with Pentecost and Easter and for more than three centuries took primacy over Christmas. However, the disputes surrounding the divinity of Christ in the fourth to the sixth century led to a greater emphasis being placed upon Christmas, a feast that emphasised God becoming incarnate in our world.

When we think of the Epiphany we are inclined to think solely of the coming of the Kings to Bethlehem. Whilst this is part of the Epiphany, or manifestation, that we celebrate on that day it is also important that we recognise that there are three manifestations of the Godhead that we celebrate on that day: The baptism of Jesus in the Jordan, the marriage feast of Canna and the coming of the Magi or Kings. All of these manifestations of the Divine are the mythic representations of an event that is constantly being repeated in human life – the Divine is to be made manifest in and through us.

We, like the Magi, can have ideas where the Divine is to be found and, like them, search in the wrong place. In the story of the Magi a great King is manifested to them in the form of a helpless child. The one we desire to find is to be found in the simple and ordinary things of life, for God always approaches us from below. This revelation runs contrary to the majority of ideas we have and thus, in our desire to find the Divine, we fail to see him. We, like the Magi, are inclined to look in the palace of our own thoughts and expectations rather than in the stable of our own lives for the one we desire.

As I have said in previous letters and talks what is most needed in our world is the ability to see, to see what is actually before us. For us to see the "Godly" requires not effort but the ability to see the Divine in the most ordinary and even unpleasant of situations or people. "All things were made through him" writes Saint John. Everything in our world both reveals and conceals the Divine and the Feast of the Epiphany challenges us to see the sacramentality of creation and recognise that there is nothing that is not his Epiphany, a manifestation of the Divine. To do this requires a certain single-mindedness of purpose, a focussing of attention, and a sense of hope that is almost alien to our culture. The Eucharist, the revelation of God in sacrament, shows that the entire world is sacramental and is therefore an unfolding of eternity in time.

Despite all our crassness, distractibility and foolishness our origins are divine and that divinity is constantly trying to manifest itself and work for a better ordering of our world. Our humanness is the form in which the Divine is made manifest and so, just as Jesus at the Jordan heard the words, "This is my beloved son in whom I am well pleased", we too need to hear these words and believe them to be true for us also. We do not have to do anything to get God on our side, we simply have to realise our worth. Only if we are able to realise this for ourselves will we be able to behave morally well; we don't become worthy because we behave well, this is the mistake of the Pharisees, but because we are worthy there are things in our life that we just don't do. The humility of God is such that the only way he can become manifest in our world is if we acquiesce to his "becoming" in us and manifesting himself in and through the things we do. "Behold I am making all things new" (Rev.21:5) is not a future promise but a description of the ongoing work of God in and through his people.

At this time of writing there are so many people responding generously to the calamity caused by the tsunami in the East. Some will have an active, a "front line" role; others will be less active but in compassion hold the dead and afflicted in their hearts whilst helping materially in whatever way they can. The task for all of us is that of bringing about a new order, a new way of living and being, by manifesting the compassion of God in Christ. How's that for a New Year resolution?

I wish you all a very Happy New Year and ask you to keep me in your heart as I keep you in mine.

My Dear Friends,
        So much seems to have happened in my world since my last letter. One of the things I wrote about at some length was the way in which I felt it necessary to involve myself in the cause of victims of asbestos related diseases. Since the time of my last letter I am pleased to report that some politicians now seem to have developed an increasing sensitivity to the problem. In due course, I would expect others, such as politicians, unions and the Scottish asbestos charities, to pick up the baton and run with it but for the moment it is essential that I do what I can to attempt to establish justice and support for those whom society is prone to overlook.

Over the last few weeks, there have been two principle "events" that have touched me deeply. One of these events was the death of Sr. Mary of the Child Jesus, an elderly Carmelite Nun and the second was a slight degree of discomfort in my back due to the development of my cancer.

I have known Sr. Mary for some twenty years and known her well for the last fifteen of those years. Like me, she was born in Lancashire and received her education in that same county. She entered Carmel at a very early age and after the closure of two Carmels in England transferred to Glasgow Carmel, where she lived for forty six years of her more than sixty years of religious consecration. I do not think that I have ever met a person who was so aptly named as she, a reflection that I often shared with her. Throughout the time I knew her she had the trust, loving affection and wonderment of a child, qualities she lived throughout the whole of her life. In some persons the above could be based upon a foolish naivety or a desire not to "grow up" and be responsible. However, in Mary nothing could be further from the truth for combined with the above qualities there was a steeliness and tenacity that would enable her to get things done yesterday! These gifts were soon spotted and utilised within Carmel for she occupied a position of responsibility within the various monasteries in which she lived from the age of twenty three, only "retiring" when she was in her eighties! Her childlikeness was no evasion but something that was part of who she genuinely was, this coupled with a sense of humour that can only be described as "impish" delighted all who met her no matter how brief that contact might be.

In the course of my working life as a therapist I have met many religious whose natures have been deformed through silly and over scrupulous regimes within religious orders; people whose ability to love and be loved were denied. Mary lived through those times of restriction but her steely qualities prevented her from abdicating responsibility for who and what she was and so retained her childlike sense of trust in the basic goodness of herself and others. The easing of foolish restrictions in the enclosed life of Carmel allowed more of her natural self to flourish and I recall once getting a Christmas card from her, when she was in her eighties, in which she wrote, "Ever since I have known you I have grown younger and younger!" A person such as she who exudes life brings life to others and so she was an ideal person to become novice mistress, a task in which she particularly excelled. Throughout the whole of her life she always had a love of young people and would delight in their presence.

Several years ago, after we had been speaking about death, she asked me if I would preach at her funeral. This I readily agreed to do, both of us assuming she would pass to the "further shore" before me. When she found out that I was terminally ill it was a grievous blow to her emotionally and spiritually causing her to think that something had gone "wrong". I suppose that it is like the agonies a parent suffers when their child dies before them; events don't make sense and feels as if something has gone wrong in the ordering of the world. To the end of her life she was convinced that God would bring about a cure of my illness and restore me to health; so certain was she about this that she found it difficult to even conceive that this might not happen. Mary's health was quite good for a woman of her age but towards the end of her life, she began to develop a series of infections that necessitated hospitalisation. These periods of hospitalisation upset her greatly for she hated to be separated from her beloved sisters, the majority of whom she had received into the Order. Like many elderly people, she also found being in hospital somewhat confusing, a fact that was not aided by being partially deaf. Her life ended very peacefully during one of these hospital confinements in the company of the Prioress and several members of the community.

Sister Mary died on the feast of St. Kentigern, the 13th of January. St. Kentigern is the patron and founder of the City of Glasgow, Mary's adopted home. Kentigern is also know as St. Mungo: the name Mungo being a name bestowed upon him by his mentor St. Serf. The name Mungo has several possible meanings but the one that most commentators agree with is "dearest friend". When I heard of Mary's death on that day I thought how appropriate it was that one who had been a "dearest friend" to so many in the city of St Kentigern should die on that day. I am pleased to say that before her death Mary had left a note to say that I was to preach at her funeral: a task that I was very willing and ready to undertake as a final act of loving service to a "dearest friend".

To preach on death when one is dying oneself is not perhaps the easiest of tasks but when the church is full of people who are also aware that one is gently crumbling this further adds to the difficulties. I do not think that I have ever felt so anxious about speaking in public but I knew that above all else I wanted to say something that would be meaningful to Mary and all those, like myself, who loved her.

Throughout our life, dying is the price we pay for an enhanced life and so when someone dies, though it is natural to feel that our world has been torn asunder, we need to recognise that nothing has "gone wrong". Grieving over our loss is right and appropriate for unless we grieve we cannot emotionally let go of the beloved but this is only part of our reality. Without death there cannot be a resurrection to a more comprehensive form of existence. As the poet Sylvia Plath once wrote, "dying is an art"; an art that we need to learn in the midst of life not simply on an occasion when we have a brush with death. Even if you have very limited self knowledge you will be aware of a tendency to try to get life on your own terms, to live an autonomous way of life in which you are firmly in control of life's events. We all have a tendency to place ourselves at the centre of life and attempt to order things to suit our preferences. Death is a reminder of the impossibility of such a way of living as it pulls us up sharp when we realise that we are not the all powerful beings we sometimes feel ourselves to be.

In our physical death, we will step out of our body but death is only a separation of our deep identity, which is rooted in God, from the physical body: The outer form passes away but the "Is-ness" of us continues to live, as an ever evolving, ever changing entity for God is not fixed or static. Everything and everybody is the twinkle of the Divine as It manifests itself within us and in creation. For this evolution to take place, it is essential that in this life we learn to appreciate the gifts given, including life itself, and then a preparedness to let go of the gift given at the appropriate time. Circumstances teach us that all we cling to will destroy us and to learn this is to reduce the pain of life and growth. The food and water upon which we are dependent will kill us if a process of elimination does not complement the intake of these things. Life is a gift given but a gift that we need to offer back to God so that the gift which was finite when given becomes in the offering back an infinite gift. Dying and rising are part of the structural principles of our world and to co-operate with them is to minimise our suffering and provide us with the least waste of human effort. Some would have it that death begins after life but this is not true: when life stops so does death.

At this time in my life, issues of life and death have an importance and a clarity that they have never had before. As I said at the beginning of this letter, a few weeks ago I began to feel some discomfort in my chest and it was recommended that I seek an earlier appointment with my oncologist. I suppose I had been weaned into a false sense of security by earlier statements to the effect that I might well have another year of life in me that I had forgotten medical interventions might be needed to improve the quality of my life. During my appointment with the oncologist it was thought that chemotherapy might be helpful for symptom control of the side effects of the mesothelioma. Looked at in this way I feel it would be foolish of me not to at least try this form of therapy. However, I am not looking forward to the treatment, though I am assured that it should not cause too much personal discomfort or encumbrance to my lifestyle. It is recommended that I have four treatments, each of which will necessitate an overnight stay in hospital, at approximately four weekly intervals. All of this assumes that I am found to be a suitable candidate for the treatment and that I will continue the treatment after the first session.

The discomfort I felt in my back a couple of weeks ago was a further reminder of how I am in the grip of a "process" over which I have absolutely no control. Each time I go to the hospital and look at my chest x-rays with the consultant I note the steady and relentless way the cancer grips more and more of my left lung, slowly squeezing the oxygen of life from me. As well as having some slight discomfort to contend with I have also been made very aware of my failing health by the winds that have buffeted the shores of Scotland. These gales have made walking my dog something of an endurance test rather than a pleasure and thus engendered in me the feeling of being frail. Of all the things I have had to contend with this is perhaps one of the more difficult because of being so fit. Within me there is a dreadful clash between an image of a former self and the reality of my present self.

On a recent trip to London I went to the nearest underground station only to find out that the lifts to the platform were not working. Since I had to walk down the stairs to the platform this was not a problem but on the way back home I found myself feeling slightly anxious and reflecting on what I would do if they had not been repaired. Not too long ago

I used to use the spiral staircases at the underground stations as part of my fitness programme by running up and down them! I mention the above to illustrate how we are inclined to cling to images of past realities and people thus making so much pain for ourselves. Without doubt, serenity lies in being able to both see and accept reality as it presents itself at each and every moment of our lives. If we struggle to escape from our own reality and attempt to get rid of whatever it is that feels to be afflicting us we create more problems further down the road. The alternative is to listen to where Life has us and acknowledge our reality and embark upon a different journey to the one we have been on. If we can acknowledge and accept our present reality then we will gain internal freedom, lessen tension and pressures. Thus we will be better able to focus upon our Primary Task which is that of "Being Christ Today". It is by accepting and even welcoming the evening years of life that we have opportunity to live our dying; that is surrender "what was" and embrace "what is"; recognising that "what is" is dynamic and ever changing. To cling to anything, anyone or the various strategies for happiness that we devise is to diminish who and what we could be, but cling we do and in the clinging make our own pain. The phrase that suits all occasions is, "And this too will pass" since it is suitable for occasions of both joy and pain, in other words it is rooted in the dynamism of Creation.

Please keep me in your heart in prayer as I keep you all in mine. Every good wish to you all.

My Dear Friends,

I write to you having undergone the first of four chemotherapy sessions which I hope will improve the quality of my living and ease my eventual demise. It is impossible for me to compare how the illness would or would not progress with or without chemotherapy, all one can do is put ones faith in those who have more experience of the condition than I. A recent scan indicated that there is severe plural thickening on the apex of my left lung: adjacent to this site are many nerve cells. It is hoped that the chemotherapy will contain and possibly reduce the spread of the cells for; left to there own devices, they could create quite a lot of pain. My consultant suggested that the discomfort I had felt in my chest a few weeks ago had to do with this plural thickening. If the chemotherapy does not do what is hoped, it is suggested that I undertake a course of radiotherapy to reduce the plural thickening. After my next chemotherapy session, scheduled for the 16/17th of March, I will have another scan to determine the next stage of my treatment.

Life and death are very much to the forefront of my mind. The process that has me within its grip revolves around the actual process of living and dying. Almost all normal cells in the body grow and die in a controlled way through a process called apoptosis. Cancer cells, on the other hand, keep dividing and forming more cells without a control mechanism to induce normal apoptosis. The anti cancer drugs used in chemotherapy destroys cancer cells by stopping them from growing or dividing at one or more points in their growth cycle. Cancer cells are cells that fail to observe the cycle of growth and death that is intrinsic to the proper ordering of the world.

With the first chemotherapy treatment I felt that another stage on the journey of letting go was reached: a stage where the management of symptoms has become both primary and necessary. Perhaps it is because we are in the season of Lent and fast approaching Holy Week that I am so very conscious of the battle between life and death. It is a process in which death will eventually have its way with me in its own time but till then I want to live my life as vibrantly as possible. Insofar as it is possible I would want my surrender to the inevitable to be both free and conscious, rather than be attenuated by a clouding of consciousness arising from opiate based medications. That is why I am undergoing chemotherapy and will, if necessary, utilise other means, such as radiotherapy, to keep the use of all my faculties for as long as I can. Being pain free is important to me not just because I am afraid of pain, which I am, but also because continual pain or distress keeps one focused upon oneself which prevents one from making that "great surrender" of which our physical dissolution is but an outward sign.

One of the decisions I made whilst in hospital was that of deciding that I did not wish to be resuscitated if my heart should stop. Should this happen to me I would consider that God was calling me home, albeit a little earlier than I had expected! I do know that I am on a journey to the Further Shore and, to me, the manner of my going seems more important than its timing. As you will possibly appreciate from the tenor of this letter I do not so much feel as if I am celebrating Lent and Holy Week as living it.

The human condition means that our needs are always beyond our capacity to meet them. We can only find the comfort and security we need if we can develop a taste for insecure living. In the game of life we have two choices, that of accepting our poverty or becoming a slave of anxiety as we try to foolishly create our own security. In the end perhaps all we can do is embrace whatever reality that confronts us with as much faith and courage as we can muster realising that there is a Power that is for us but not of us.

A good number of years ago whilst on a bus going to Manchester from my home town of Leigh I noticed a sign outside of a Methodist Church. The sign said, "Don't just do something, sit there". The sentiments behind those words have always remained with me though initially I found the idea very puzzling. I often think that the bravest thing we can do is remain where we are when everything in us aches to do something: it doesn't matter what we do, anything will suffice just so long as it gets us away from the feeling of helplessness that induces panic.

A number of years ago I was in the Daughters of Saint Paul's bookshop in Glasgow when I noticed a guide to the Holy Land by Jerome Murphy O'Connor, a Dominican biblical scholar. Having recently read an article by him I was interested in his guide to the Holy Land. As I picked up the book it opened at the page devoted to the Garden of Gethsemane. The descriptions of the location were as precise as one would expect of a biblical scholar who not only lives in but loves the Holy Land. However, the thing that I particularly remember was his assertion that Jesus, with just half an hour's brisk walk, could have escaped into the wilderness.

Reading this made me realise that perhaps the bravest thing we can ever do is to stay still, stand our ground, when everything in us wants to run away, to do something to escape the panic that almost overwhelms us. It is in moments of aloneness that our minds lack surety and we crave the outer security that deep down we know is illusion. The sad truth is that there is nothing outside of ourselves that we can depend upon and to put our faith in objects that are unworthy of our faith is, eventually, the cause of great hurt. The only security that is offered to us is to put our hand in the hand of the One who can never be known other than through love. The problem with this God is that he is the eleventh hour God; a God who always comes at the moment when our own resources have failed. We have no alternative other than to put our trust in him if we are to get away from the obsessive rumination over the troubles that afflict us but despite this knowledge we all too often prefer our self obsessed ponderings to becoming free.

Love is the subordinating of our self to Something and it is only through recognising that, ultimately, we don't have a choice as to how we can live our lives if we are to live with a degree of authenticity. We may hesitate to choose, thus prolonging our pain, but if we are to be authentic we must, like Jesus in the Garden, finally utter the terrible words, "Thy will not my will be done". In our modern world the inability to choose to live by That which is essential for our existence is called freedom – a reversal of the truth. True freedom is the freedom to focus down from many choices to the object of love that we call God. This is a way of being that abolishes distance between self and Other and a unity of wills is achieved. As the story of Jesus in the Garden clearly displays this process is not devoid of pain nor is it something that can be achieved once and for all. The human person is capable of infinite expansion and so we have never "arrived", become "enlightened", there is always more to be given, more to be transformed in us.

A prayer in the Iona Community Worship book refers to Jesus as "the Master Craftsman", one who has the capacity to make something new out of those who come "rough hewn" to his bench. For human nature to be restored, for people to stop living at arm's length from God, the love of God has to show itself alive even in distress and agony, in the darkness of suffering and dying. A God that shrinks away from our greatest fears and trials is not worthy of our veneration for Love must go to a place where one would not expect to find it. That is why Jesus meets his death on the cross, an instrument of torture, on the city rubbish heap. It had to be this painful and humiliating if nowhere and no one are to be closed off from God. Christ's life is not simply a historical fact for by his death and resurrection he inaugurated a way of Being. Having his Spirit, our task is that of being Christ today.

How ironic it is that at the moment of his crucifixion St. John writes of Jesus being "glorified": at this the moment of his greatest degradation. At the time when he is furthest away from peace, wellbeing and success he achieves his purpose as he hands over his life to his God and gives his Spirit to those who believe in him (Jn 19:30). Because we are inheritors of that Spirit whenever God sees us he sees his own beloved Son whose life is now totally interwoven with ours.

The obedience to the will of the Father that Jesus manifested is only of value insofar as we share in that way of being he came to inaugurate. How quickly the words, "Thy will be done" slip off the tongue without us realising that those words are not so much a prayer as an offering of self. For Christ saves us from our troubles by annihilating the egotism that keeps us separate from the Divine and asserting a true selfhood that comes from acceptance of God's will. There really is only one prayer, the prayer of Christ, a continuous offering of self that culminates in the Cross. That is why it is essential that we stop thinking about prayer as being "my" prayer and see it more as a way to the Father, through the Son in the Spirit.

It is quite common amongst Christians to hear that Jesus had it much easier than you and I; he knew all would be well in the end. Lying behind this supposition is the idea that Jesus was not really a man but God dressed up as man. However, Christian tradition would have it that he was fully man and thus would have the same fears as you and I. In the same way he had to become conscious, as you and I have to, of the Divine Life within him. He had to become not only conscious of the powerful mystery that holds all things in being but, in acts of surrender, to allow this Mystery to be central to his existence. He did this by creating a space within him so as to become conscious of the Divine, then live in obedience to It.

One of the events I eagerly anticipate this Easter is the reception of a good friend into the Roman Catholic Church. My eagerness has nothing to do with the zeal for converts. I would have been equally happy to see him become a committed member of another faith should that have been his calling but this was not the case. Throughout my life I have always tried to live from within myself and in my life and teaching encourage others to do the same. The principle reason for my rejoicing is that I have seen someone struggle against both the need to belong and the fear of belonging. This is a struggle that has been played itself out in his life for twenty years or so. In his enthusiasm he has initially given himself to the Church, been frightened of the commitment and then withdrawn. Such a process is almost built into human nature as we make grand gestures, then frighten ourselves and retract the gift of self. Jesus' Agony in the Garden is a wonderful portrayal of humanity wrestling with itself and convinces us that the Crucified is no stranger to us but one whose life provides a commentary on our own.

Christian commitment, the following of Christ, means an "about turn" of the whole being in its depths. If this is not the case the baptism which accompanies it is mere ceremonial. Because it does cause a complete upheaval it is a commitment that we wrestle with throughout our lives. It is impossible to tuck ones Christianity into a quiet corner of one's life and simply put it on each and every Sunday. It is this caricature of Christianity that causes people to halt at the door of our churches. But true Christianity confronts a man with himself, in the nakedness of his being, and sets him face to face with his God. All too often Christians believe, not in Jesus, but in some "idea" of a saviour, a product of their own mind that they can have control over.

Many people these days speak of having "lost their faith" but it is impossible to lose an authentic faith. A faith that has opened up the very centre of the personality to the action of the Spirit can never be lost, only one founded on illusion can be lost. Christianity involves a repeated letting go of all that is ephemeral and unreal and thus always involves pain and loss but the letting go is always a death to life experience. If one has an authentic faith one may question but what will be questioned will always be the external expressions of ones inner faith, never the faith itself. It saddens me deeply that people mistake the outward "form" of religion for the reality of faith; as if religion was an idea rather than an experience. They fail to recognise that it is essential to go beyond ideas and words to Reality itself if one is to have faith rather than belief.

No Christian will ever know peace until he or she accepts the need to change, accepts their fundamental insecurity and their inability to order the world in the way they would choose. As well as this they need to know that they will be called to live heroically at some time in their life and that this time will not be of their choosing. But when that is done there is no other simpler and freer way of living for they know that in everything the Father's love is being displayed. This surely is the message of Holy Week and Easter?

May this special time of the Churches year be for you a time of new beginnings and fecundity of Life. Please keep me in your heart as I shall keep you in mine.

My Dear Friends,

So much has happened since my last letter to you that it is difficult to know where to begin. Perhaps the most obvious subject to begin with is the death of my dog Barclay. It was during Holy Week that it proved necessary to terminate his life, a season that seemed most appropriate to such a loss. For some years he had problems with the vertebrae in his neck but in times past, with rest and the use of anti-inflammatory drugs, he always got better. In his final illness this was not the case and so I felt compelled to make the decision I did. Given that he had been my constant companion for nine years the decision was not arrived at without the most enormous amount of distress. When I telephoned the veterinarian to ask him to come and put the dog down, initially, I could not say why I was 'phoning due to being wracked with sobs. The only thing that gave me the courage to say the words was the degree of distress the dog was in and the look of anguish in his eyes as he looked to me for comfort in his pain.

When I got him nine years ago he was a nervous wreck having been treated harshly. He was so nervous he had to be persuaded to walk down stairs; so much so that when he came down the stairs he would shake with anxiety. Barclay was also apprehensively aggressive towards men and would growl whenever he met a man and back away from them. All of these behaviours took a while to overcome but in the end he became the fun loving creature that God made him to be. I think that all dog owners and parents believe their dog or child is special in some way or other. I am happy to confess that I am no different than anyone else in this matter. One of the things I will always remember about him was his adoring gaze as he would look at me. For many years my prayer has been, "Lord help me to be the person my dog thinks I am".

His going has left an enormous gap in my life but along with my grief is a sense of freedom. My greatest concern on hearing that I had a terminal condition was not how long I had to live but what would happen to Barclay when I became too ill to look after him. Knowing how messed up psychologically he was when first I got him my fear was that of him ending his days in a similar psychological condition to the one he had when I inherited him. This situation was ameliorated by friends saying that they would care for him when I was no longer able to do so and for that I was truly grateful, knowing that they would care for him as much as I did. However, I also knew that at some time in the future I would have to take him to their house, turn my back on him and leave him with them knowing full well that I would never be able to see him again: as you can imagine this was not a thought I relished.

By whatever means I knew that one day I would have to lose him and of the two options losing him to death now feels to be the easier way. In holding him as life flowed out of his body I was able to perform my last duty of care and know that a chapter of life had ended for both of us. His passing could not have been more peaceful or tranquil and with his demise I felt, along with great sadness, a sense of freedom. What I had dreaded had now been confronted and I had survived the loss, albeit feeling a little knocked about emotionally.

I realise full well that this "letting go" is only one of a series of "little deaths" that will face me in the not too distant future as my health deteriorates and so it felt quite appropriate that Barclay's death should have taken place on the day before Good Friday. As I said to a number of people at the time, "I don't so much feel that I am celebrating Holy Week as living it". To become like Jesus in his death, his desolation, is the highest state that a person can ascribe to attain. This conformity with Jesus in his abandonment on the cross is the very precondition for mystical prayer, for Jesus is not so much an object of our devotion as our inmost essence.

In the person of Christ on the cross we see one who is totally free; one stripped of family, friends, reputation, life and even a sense of the Father's presence. But stripped of all the things that we tend to cling to he is totally free and available to the Father, which is, of course, what we are called to be. The letting go of words, symbols, feelings Saint John of the Cross calls the "dark night of the soul" whilst Jesus calls it "losing one's life". In his writings John of the Cross argues that the redemption of the world is grounded in the dying of one's peripheral self as one embraces the path of deep prayer.

In the "Ascent of Mount Carmel" (Book 2 , Chapter 7-11) he writes:
"At the moment of his death he was certainly annihilated in his soul, without any consolation or relief, since the Father left him that way in innermost aridity in the lower part. He was thereby compelled to cry out: My God, My God, why have you forsaken me? (Mt27:46) This was the most extreme abandonment, sensitively, that he had suffered in his life. And by it he accomplished the most marvellous work of his whole life, surpassing all the works, deeds and miracles that he had ever performed on earth or in heaven. That is, he brought about the reconciliation and union of the human race with God through grace. The Lord achieved this, as I say, at the moment in which he was most annihilated in all things: in his reputation before men, since in beholding him die they mocked him instead of esteeming him; in his human nature, by dying; and in spiritual help and consolation from his Father, for he was forsaken by his Father at that time to bring men to union with God.........The journey, then does not consist in recreation, experiences, and spiritual feelings, but in the living, sensory and spiritual, exterior and interior death of the cross."
To become like Jesus in this annihilation is the highest state the soul can reach and consists of experiencing the death on the cross emotionally, spiritually, inwardly and outwardly.

Just as Jesus manifested divine life in his humanity, we too have to manifest divine life in our humanity. This requires us to love our humanity for it is the means by which Divinity expresses itself in us. We are most aware of this Presence when we live fully our inner emptiness and renounce the things we are inclined to cling to. However, our goal is not renunciation and emptiness for they are only a prerequisite for resurrection and new life; it is a death to life experience. Invariably circumstances will come into our lives when, with as much good grace as we can muster, we will be asked to surrender what we have in order to savour a newness, a transformation, of being, an experience of resurrection.

In my last letter I wrote of a friend who was to be received into the Church during the Easter Vigil. The service was wonderful and possibly all the more wonderful for my wondering if it would be the last opportunity I would have to celebrate the Easter mysteries. Once again I was struck by the dynamism of the Christian faith that requires us to let go of what we have in order to inherit newness of life and fullness of being: to put behind one the circumstances of the past and embrace a new Reality. Our purification, liberation and the unmasking of the many illusions that we are prey to are essential tasks on the journey of faith. Part of the Vigil service is the renewing of baptismal promises where we promise to renounce Satan and all his "works and pomps". We require faith to believe that all evil is reversible and can be changed to good by love and forgiveness along with sufficient humility to believe that no sin committed can be as strong as God's love.

It is only those who have begun to see through loving eyes, with the eyes of God, who will be able to provide the necessary resistance to evil without becoming the mirror image of that which they oppose. This is so because they are rooted in a power that is greater than them and so they are not swayed or deflected by humiliation or honour. Authentic spirituality is not a search for consolation or comfort, or inner peace, though these things may come as a result of the spiritual search, but a quest for Truth. Simone Weil once wrote (Gateway to God p56): "love is not consolation but light, religion insofar as it is a source of consolation is a hindrance to true faith. In this sense, atheism is a purification".

Death and resurrection are but one moment in time. It is in "dying" to our dignity, power, and success, being highly thought of, that we pass beyond the peripheral and illusory to root ourselves in the abiding love of God. Life in its many and varied aspects is filled with many small deaths and resurrections all of which serve to prepare us for our physical dissolution. However, our physical death is but a sign of the spiritual death necessary to be like Jesus; totally open, totally free.

You might be tempted to wonder why all this talk of death and surrender is to the forefront of my mind. I think that this is the case due to my having to be hospitalised the other week after developing a throat infection. My immune system was so low at the time that I was unable to fight off the infection with oral antibiotics and had to be admitted to hospital where I was given intravenous antibiotics. There was nothing life threatening about the procedure or the event but it reminded me very forcefully that one day something like this will happen and I will be unable to slough off the infection. As I understand it, cancers are seldom the cause of a person's death; generally it is caused by infections that arise as a result of deficiencies in the immune system. Last week's hospital admission was the harbinger of how things will be from now on – periods of wellbeing punctuated by periods of illness and symptom control.

However, I am glad to say that for the moment at least I am well, free from pain, able to eat and in good spirits! One thing that life has taught me of late is to rejoice in the simplest of thing like feeling hungry and eating without discomfort, being pain free and having energy. These gifts we are inclined to take for granted and forget that they are gifts to be rejoiced in so don't forget to celebrate having a day free from discomfort! But its not only in this matter I consider myself to be fortunate because I am supported by the love and prayers of so many good people whose cards, calls, and assurances of prayer are such a support.

I never cease to marvel at the goodness of people and constantly am surprised at their generosity of spirit. A small illustration of people's goodness would be the ceilidh organised by a couple of friends to support the work of asbestos charities in Scotland, one of which has appointed me a director. This initiative undertaken by just two people soon attracted the attention of others and soon numerous others were involved. Many made donations, offered prizes, petitioned their companies to support the causes, offered their skills and talents and actively promoted the event amongst their friends and colleagues. The event raised some £2,000 but perhaps the most important thing was that many more people became conscious of the pain and distress that can be caused by these asbestos related illnesses. Education seldom goes hand in hand with pleasure but on this occasion I am led to believe that everyone had a wonderful evening with great music, food and drink. Well done to all involved!

Keep me in your heart as I keep you in mine.

My Dear Friends,

I know that it is not very long since my last letter to you but as you know these letters are written as and when I feel inspired, if that is the right word, to do so. One of the reasons I am writing so soon has to do with the fact of my feeling well and full of energy. My course of chemotherapy has ended and I find myself no more breathless than I was several months ago. Due to treatments I have had, life has not been easy lately but that now seems to have passed and, for the moment at least, life is relatively good. In short, my condition is said to be "stable", a fact verified by a recent scan.

The week before Pentecost we had a celebration of the sacrament of the sick during Sunday mass at my parish in Tayport. As you will know from my letters I have received this sacrament on several occasions since the diagnosis of terminal cancer was made. When names of those desiring the sacrament were asked for I found myself somewhat reluctant to put my name forward. The reason for this had to do with my publicly having to identify myself as being one of the "sick". The inclusion of this sacrament within the regular Sunday mass was very special and the silence of the congregation during the imposition of hands was what the Society of Friends might describe as "a gathered silence": a selfless silence that can only come as a result of flowing out to the other. Those of us who were recipients of the sacrament were held in the hearts and minds of all present in such an inclusive way as to re-enforce our belonging to the corporate body of both Church and parish.

The healing power of the Spirit of Jesus is still with his Church just as it was in apostolic times. Because every object every person is shot through with the grace of God, the Church is not afraid to use the things of the world to aid us in our journey towards God. Thus it is that the Church uses oil as a sacramental sign of its love and desire to bring healing to the one who is ill. Similarly, the Church may use the practice of blessing the sick person with objects that symbolise the power of God.

Prior to the actual anointing with the oil I found myself very easily moved and on several occasions my eyes were pricked by tears. This had to do with admitting my vulnerability and need of healing. I have never found it easy to be "looked after" and always maintained a fierce independence, often to my own damage and the hurt of friends. During the mass I was surprised at the level of anxiety I experienced prior to my anointing with oil, I was afraid of being the centre of attention and being seen as one of "the sick".

After I had been anointed the anxiety faded away and though I know my cancer is still with me I feel that I was the recipient of healing on that day. The healing that took place was a healing within my heart that enabled me to be who I was and how I was. For healing in depth, rather than the simple amelioration of symptoms, we need to abdicate the control we feel we have over our lives and the image of how we "ought" to be. That Sunday I learned a little more how to be the person I am by letting go of false images of me and accommodating to a new reality and new needs.

The great sacrament of everyday healing is the Eucharist; which so powerfully expresses our desire to "share in the divinity of him who came to share in our humanity" (Roman Liturgy). Because the Eucharist, like all sacraments, takes us beyond ourselves into the Godhead it has the capacity to unite us through the healing of all that afflicts us and separates us from each other and from God. The diversity of personalities within the average church congregation never ceases to amaze me. This variety is not solely centred upon personality but also upon preferences with regard to liturgical style. For example, we may or may not like the hymns chosen; the degree of silence or lack of it; the manner of the priest who presides. All of us very different but here we are each Sunday being the happy, struggling, content, offended, raw, puzzled people we are in a scandal ridden church that so often seems to thrive upon abuse of power and authority. Some, or most of us, don't even know each other and perhaps that is as well for if we did we might not even like each other!

Despite who and how we are the Spirit of God is just as much around us as it was at Pentecost and nothing can prevent it from blowing through each of us and all of us whenever this diverse group of people are together. Like those at the first Pentecost, despite all the differences, we have a deeper union "and one Spirit was given to us all to drink" (1Cor 12:13). It is this Spirit which urges us ever onwards to a new mode of being by forcing us out of the narrow and confined space that we live in so that we can take wings and fly.

Today there are many who no longer feel the need of Church belonging or liturgical celebrations. The rituals of Church are no longer seen as being necessary for life and living; seen to be boring and not make much sense. However, there is a sense in which, when you explain the liturgy, it is not the liturgy anymore. To explain liturgy is like trying to explain a poem: if the meaning the poem is carrying could be completely explained, then there would be no need to write the poem in the first place!! The written liturgy, like a good poem, is a term of reference; the experience is beyond words. The words and the rituals aren't necessarily our teachers; they are the means of access to the Teacher, for the Teacher is the lived experience. In that sense, the liturgy is ultimately silent.

It is interesting that in the earliest days of the Church, a person was taught the Lord's Prayer late in their preparation for reception into the Church. This was also true of teachings on the Christian mysteries such as the Holy Trinity and those concerning the Virgin Mary. The symbolism of the Eucharist is very powerful indeed but the meaning is all too often lost under a welter of words that almost prevent transcendent experience. You just can't tell someone everything all at once. Intellectually he or she cannot bear it, because they, as yet, have not had the illuminative experience that allows them to see.

I believe that the practice of contemplative prayer is the greatest aid there is in enabling people to see: to see what is there, not what you think is there, ought to be there, but what actually is there! But along with the practice of the prayer of quiet is the need to be part of a praying community. It is a humbling experience to know one's need of fellowship and whilst some may be called, like Simone Weil, to live a separate autonomous kind of Christianity most will have to learn to embrace and learn to love it in its more mundane and difficult manifestations.

I think that the thing I learned from my experience of the sacrament of the sick was that I very much belong to this needy, flawed and very fallible group called the Church. At times I wish it were otherwise but this is the place that has brought me life and hope, a place that has brought me greater personal growth than I ever imagined possible in an institution that I both love and hate. Such experiences as the one I write of convince me of where I belong and how I belong and thus both a comfort and a challenge.

My Dear Friends,

In my last letter to you I stated that my health was stable and I am happy to report that this still seems to be the case. Given my present state of health I have been rejoicing in having both the health and stamina to visit people and places. It is now fourteen months since I was diagnosed as suffering from mesothelioma and given between six and eighteen months to live. Well, it seems as though I am going to live a little longer than expected! This period of my life is especially fecund and I thank God for each and every day. As some of you will know I have recently returned from my holiday in the City of York, a city that has a special place in my heart. As always, I found myself moved by the magnificence of the Minster, which incidentally contains the greatest expanse of medieval glass in the world. Listening to Evensong in the Minster increases ones sense of wonderment and joy in that splendid building. As the choir sang I wondered how the master masons managed to build a structure with such wonderful acoustics. It is difficult enough today to build a building with good acoustics with all the technological aids presently available so I just can't imagine how they managed to do this!

Towards the latter part of my stay in that city I made several visits to a smaller and humbler church, the Parish Church of St. Martin le Grand, Coney Street, York. This church was founded in the late 1000s, extensively rebuilt in the 1400, and was badly damaged by enemy action in 1942. In 1968 the church was partially restored as a chapel and garden of peace, and rededicated as: "a shrine of remembrance for all who have died in two wars, a chapel of peace and reconciliation between nations and men". It is also significant that St. Martin, who is the patron saint of soldiers, has his feastday on the 11th of November which is, as I am sure you will remember, Armistice Day.

A few weeks before going on holiday I went to see a friend who is Director of The St. Ethelburga's Centre for Reconciliation and Peace, 78, Bishopsgate, London. In 1993, a bomb exploded in Bishopsgate partially destroying the small medieval church of St. Ethelburga. The church was very badly damaged but has been rebuilt and serves as an important symbol of hope in the heart of the city. It is a venue for dialogue between groups in conflict both at home and from overseas. It helps analyse the role of religions in international affairs and seeks to further the contribution that faith communities can make to preventing deadly conflict. It is a living memorial to the men and women who have dedicated their lives to the pursuit of peace". If you would like more information on the work done in the Centre you can find details at http://www.stethelburgas.org .

It was soon after my visit to St Ethelburga's that a bombing campaign began in London that has shocked not only Londoners but the entire world. Sometimes when I read a newspaper or watch the news of the bombings and attempted bombings on television I do not particularly like the sentiments that I experience. Herein lies the problem, if we are to stop wars we must start with our own hearts and minds and the place to acquire the skills to avoid or resolve conflict is in our own homes, workplaces or any place were decisions are made.

Conflicts are inevitable and provide a means of our maturation. Therefore they should not be repressed or ignored but worked through slowly and painfully in an effort to develop consensus and, if necessary make reparation for wrongs committed. In order to mature we must learn to reject the whisperings of revenge that too readily spring up within our hearts. In a situation of conflict both sides assert claims and rights; rights to territories, property, economic benefits, opportunities, etc. Each side in the conflict easily and readily presents arguments to substantiate their claims whilst rejecting any viewpoint that contradicts these claims. It is a sad fact that when a particular interest group meets what is taken as opposition it creates a hostile image of a particular race, nation, faith or personality. These images and prejudices are popular among people of a like mind because these images, which have their roots in the deepest psychological realms of the human mind, have the capacity to generate social unity. In short, people are inclined to band together to confirm and affirm their prejudice against a faith, nation or people.

For decades there has been a situation of conflict in many parts of the world, so much so that it has proved impossible to establish peace in such regions. Why is this the case? It is very easy to say, that "the other side" doesn't really want either peace or compromise but the problem lies much deeper. We tend to blame the other for the situation of conflict and act as if we had nothing at all to do with it. Thus it is that we end up subjected to spirals of violence and counter violence: each side reacting to the suffering meted out by the other convinced that the solution will only come about when "they" come to their senses and see things our way. Left to ourselves we would favour a policy that committed us to a course of action that involves the least possible risk or change to ourselves.

Such an attitude means that we will not change our attitude or stance but expect the other to change. It is a sad reflection upon politics today that if a politician admits to changing their mind upon some subject they would be vilified by their colleagues. All too often leaders of communities state that they offer friendship and reconciliation but these statements are all too often mere propaganda as there is no intention of giving up previously stated positions, "rights", spheres of influence, etc. Negotiation or dialogue means being prepared to change your position, not weasel words designed to obfuscate. It means being prepared to abandon a position whereby one tries to dominate a situation or a group of people; of not exploiting the position of strength in which one finds oneself.

I do not believe that such attitudes can be called Christian nor can it properly be called "spiritual". I cannot speak with any authority about other faiths but as I understand it, the example of Christ would seem to indicate that we are to use the "power" we have to help the other, rather than impose our will upon them. We can attempt to impose our power upon others in a variety of ways; we can do this religiously, militarily, through acts of terrorism, or economically. Recently there was a G8 meeting at Gleneagles here in Scotland and it pleased me that so many people were ready to surrender their economic power in order to better the lives of so many others. I am not quite sure that all of them realised that this is what they were doing but surely it is a sign of hope. Power exists not for domination but for service. World leaders can only make concessions if we allow them to humanize the world, show a little compassion, by surrendering the power we in the West have over emerging economies. The alternative is to cling to our standard of living, insist that our industries and farmers are protected at no matter what cost to others.

Christianity says something that is not ordinarily found in economic text books, either of the right or left – it is wrong to exploit other people or nations. This is equally true for the politician, the employer, the trade unionist, the business man, the churchman and all who have power over others. It is foolish to say that what needs to be abolished is power because all of us, to a greater or lesser extent, have power over others; even a tiny infant. You don't believe me? Well you try ignoring the crying of a small baby and you will see how much power such a small bundle has! There is no substitute for a compassionate self knowledge coupled with a true humility; the greater the power the greater our need for humility and self knowledge.

Each of us is a victim of the prejudice we are brought up with; the attitudes and prejudices of the society in which we grew up. Just a cursory reading of the Gospels will leave one with the realisation that as a Christian one must give up prejudice and fanaticism. Prejudice and fanaticism spring from an incapacity to understand and therefore love the other. We need to remember that whilst Christ never condemned any individual he had little time for those who put their "cause" above love for the other. The world in which we live is a school in which we are to learn the art of loving; for it is this that marks us out as godlike creatures, living icons of the Divine.

Those who turn to God without turning from themselves are in danger of falling prey to evil in a variety of ways. The spiritual life is only of benefit insofar as it makes us less self absorbed, less self concerned; anything that inflates the ego runs clean contrary to authentic religion. Throughout history much mischief has been done by idealists convinced that they were acting from the very best motives. Anyone who turns towards God without turning away from their own "cause" does not, of course, get God: they may do well by the cause they espouse but their quest is not and never can be spiritual. Such people can, and often do, perpetrate hideous crimes, which their natural selves would be ashamed of, in the furtherance of their cause. However, we also need to recognise that such blindness is not simply the preserve of religionists for many people have been tortured, denied freedom, denied independence, right of expression, etc. by secular groups and authorities. Often this has been done under the banner of "revolution", "the rights of the common man", etc. We need to accept that we human beings are gregarious and will come together in some manner or other. If we do not come together in a Love that transcends difference we will band together behind ideologies and causes were we will find our unity in opposing others. Religion should be a remedy for our natural inclination to gather around totems and ideologies rather than the God of Love who holds all things in being.

However, we need to recognise that part of us delights in cultic notions of religion because we would rather not go through the alarming and unpleasant process of "dying to self" which is the precondition of entering into the Kingdom. The need for "right belief" is the first branch of the Buddhist "Eightfold Path", wrong belief is seen as the cause of bondage and ignorance. (This is a simple example of how other faiths have the capacity to validate and expand upon the truths of our own faith and thus an example of our need to be open to difference.) However, the practice of "self-sacrifice" in prayer and manner of living is a bore – it is much more interesting to argue and score points off ones opponents or indulge in what we call righteous indignation! But change we must if our faith is to be more than an ersatz faith based upon some kind of cultic and social belonging.

William Law a spiritual writer of the eighteenth century wrote the following on the practice of pseudo religion:-
"Now religion in the hands of self, or corrupt nature, serves only to discover vices of a worse kind than mature left to itself. Hence are all the disorderly passions of religious men, which burn in a worse flame than passions only employed about worldly matters; pride, self exaltation, hatred and persecution, under a cloak of religious zeal, will sanctify actions which nature, left to itself, would be ashamed to own."

Turning to God without turning away from "self" with its prejudices and strategies for happiness seems to explain all the follies of the extremist of whatever faith, denomination or social grouping. Faith and prejudice can easily be confused by anyone who does not properly understand the true nature of religion and it is only through the practice of authentic faith that observers will be able to spot the difference.

Christians like humanists' support all that is good, true, beautiful and human but not only these wonderful things but they also strive to find the "goodness" in things deemed to be negative such as pain, war, death, suffering and sin. Perhaps that is the reason why we need churches such as St. Ethelburga's and St. Martin le Grand to remind us of our inclination to use power to further the various causes we espouse. In their damaged structures they manifest the consequences of using that power and in their "new" ministries show how something good can come from a perceived "evil". Sometimes it will be necessary to "contain" wrong doing but in the containment of it we should be sure that we ourselves do not become the mirror image of what we oppose. Peace begins with me and how I resolve conflict and discord within my home, place of work, church community or any other place where decisions are made.

I would like to share this brief prayer for peace with you. It is the Universal Prayer for Peace.

> O God, lead us from death to life,
> from falsehood to truth.
> Lead us from despair to hope,
> from fear to trust.
> Lead us from hate to love,
> from war to peace.
> Let peace fill our hearts,
> our world our universe. Amen

My Dear Friends,

As far as I am aware my health remains stable. I am still pain free and able to get about without too much difficulty. In a few weeks time I am once again to see my oncologist and I will know if my condition remains stable, which I believe to be the case, or whether the cancer has started to grow again.

The past few weeks has seen me visit Iona, London and Northern Ireland twice! Apart from finding things a little more tiring than I used to there is little wrong with me. I know this sounds a strange thing to say but I find it somewhat difficult to accept being as well as I am! Let me explain, in the last few months two people who expressed sympathy over my diagnosis have themselves died of cancer. Part of me is left wondering why I am still here when others have been taken in the matter of a few months. I know that such questions are silly but nevertheless such are the thoughts that creep into my mind in the early hours of the morning. People tell me that there is still some work that I have yet to accomplish and that is why I am still here.

Such sentiment is flattering but I find it difficult to believe that I have anything special in me and so it is difficult to imagine that I have some great work to perform. I take delight in that fact of my "ordinary-ness" for therein lies the source of any gifts I have. Any worth that there has been in talks or retreats I have given have always come about as a consequence of the realisation that I am little different from the vast majority of people. The difficulties of living, of faith, the self doubt and emotional pain that comes as a result of simply living are my lot and the lot of all humanity.

One of the things that I have found both a blessing and somewhat difficult in the recent past is the way people's manner of relating changes as a consequence of my having terminal cancer. This has both positive and negative manifestations. It has lead people to express gratitude for events in the past or the warm sentiments that they have been unable to utter till now. Knowing that time is now finite they have found courage to speak secret words of affection locked in their hearts. Such expressions lead to a heightened affect in both of us. This is often quite rightly accompanied by the shedding of tears of gratitude for the gift of each other. Such sentiments invariably expand the personalities of each of us and both of us become the recipients of a new level of being. All real living is meeting, wrote Martin Buber in his spiritual classic "I and Thou". When we really meet someone else something enclosed within us is unlocked and we flow out in peace, not only to that person but to the world in general.

However, if people can't reach out in the above way it leads to uneasiness within their personality that in turn leads them to withdraw emotionally and possibly physically. This kind of reaction is not simply born of my own experience but is common to many of us who have cancer. One can know that one has not given any cause for offence but in the "wee small hours" it can feel very different. If all of us were totally secure in the conviction of our own lovability this would never be an issue but such assurance of our own lovability is impossible for most of us this side of the grave! The result of this is a feeling of rejection, an emotion so very much a part of ordinary human living.

Most of my life in the Order has been given over to helping people to see that in life we grow through pain and adversity. In my own life I recognise that the greatest lessons in living are those that are occasioned with loss and discomfort not gain and affirmation. When we feel that people have brought hurt to us it is all too easy to convince ourselves that someone has done something to us that has made us feel the pain we do. However, it is impossible to make anyone feel anything! I know that for many of you this will seem a strange concept but it is a fact! We feel the way we feel – no one has the power to control our feelings or reactions to situations. It might feel otherwise but the truth is how I react to a situation will be governed by past experience, temperament, degree of tiredness, etc. No one is powerful enough to make us feel anything.

The temptation when one feels hurt by others is to first of all determine how people "should" be and try by every imaginable strategy to bring people up to that "level". In other words one starts with the idea of how people should be and one works at changing them. It is a sad fact that most of us, rather than change ourselves, would rather put our energies into changing others and trying to influence them. This we do under the guise of "correcting" or "improving" them but in so doing we neglect our own need for an inner growth that is rooted in Christ.

Notionally, we desire change but do not see how addicted we are to our compulsions and neurotic needs for validation. It is only when we can see ourselves as we are that we can begin to change. Clarity of perception is far more important than "doing the right thing", which all too often is little other than a means of validating our own ego and "earning", through various "strategies", the love we feel we need. It is much more helpful to recognise that I do not want to change my way of living or relating because it requires me to give up various strategies that part of me believes will bring me happiness.

The sad truth is that most of us, including myself, are very self centred and so we tend to see only the suffering that is within ourselves and fail to notice the suffering that is within others. Only when you see the suffering in the person who has occasioned suffering in you can you no longer consider the person who hurt you your "enemy". When one is unhappy one's unhappiness spills over to all those around you and one then becomes inclined to try and recruit others to see your adversary in the way that you do. Thus it is that the pain you are in draws others into its spiral of negativity and hurt. By taking the focus of attention away from our own hurt and learning the art of tolerance and understanding we free ourselves from anger and the desire to retaliate.

Looking at others with compassionate eyes brings an inner peace, the ability to let go of hurt which in turn reduces suffering. We are called upon in the Gospel to "love our enemies" a task that is only possible when we can understand the other: only when you understand that your so called "enemy" suffers too can you can forgive and let go of your own hurt. Painful occasions in our life provide us with a chance to thank God for a further opportunity to gain insight and self knowledge but sadly we all too often hide away from an opportunity for growth by blaming someone else for our pain and misfortune.

The purpose of life is, first of all, good relationships with God and with other people, second, enjoying the gifts of the senses that God has given us, and third, and perhaps most important of all, to be able to actualize our own talents, so as to give as much as possible to the world around us. When we can actually give of ourselves to others, our lives are entering into the fullness of being that should be our ultimate destiny.

As some of you will be aware, in November I am due to celebrate my sixtieth birthday. It is a birthday that I never imagined I would live to see this time last year. However, here it is looming large on the horizon and I thank God for the extra time that has been given to me. Some people keep saying that the event needs to be marked in some special way. However, I would prefer it if you could simply hold me in your heart on the 9th of November, the date of my birth. I do not want any gifts as it seems inappropriate that at this stage of my life I should be acquiring things. Similarly when my energy levels are none too high it would also be silly to expect me to enjoy a party. I have never been a social animal and these days I am even less of one!

If you would like to mark the occasion in some way perhaps you could make a contribution to a charity that I am involved in, Asbestos Action Tayside. Should you wish to do this you should send your contribution to, Mr. Ian Babbs, 6, Lauder Road, Kirkcaldy, Fife, KY2 5BD and make the cheque payable to Asbestos Action Tayside. The charity aims to advise and support sufferers from asbestos related diseases and we hope to establish an office in the Dundee area in the not too distant future.

I am not sure if you will hear from be before the 9th of November but if not thank you for holding me in your prayer; I feel very much at peace about my life and my future.

My Dear Friends,

About five weeks ago I went to see my oncologist who informed me that my x-rays show my condition remains stable. Once again I received the good news that she did not want to see me for another two months unless I had pain or a dramatic change in my condition. I am pleased to say that I remain pain free and my only symptom seems to be that of having less energy than I formerly had. This kind of problem is no problem as it is easily remedied by taking the occasional nap and spending a little more time in bed, neither of which constitute a hardship! As you will appreciate, the news that my condition is stable is as good a piece of news as I can ever hope for. I have lived much longer than was expected after my initial diagnosis and to have done this with the quality of life I presently have is a wonderful gift.

Last week I celebrated my sixtieth birthday, a birthday that neither my family, my brothers in the Order nor myself expected to see. As you will know from my last letter, I did not want a celebration of the event nor did I want birthday presents because it seems silly to be accumulating things at this time of my life. The day itself I found, not surprisingly, a strange sort of day, a day that was filled with all kinds of conflicting emotions. However, things became even stranger when I checked my e-mails on my palmtop computer in Belfast City Airport. In checking my e-mails there were several wishing me a happy birthday and telling me how pleased they were that I was still around to celebrate the day. As you can imagine, I was touched by the sentiments of these communications but there was also another e-mail containing the first draft of my obituary. This was sent by a good friend who is doing me the kindness of writing my obituary for the Christian Meditation website and he had unknowingly sent this to me on my birthday so I could check the personal details. As you can possibly imagine, this generated in me a maelstrom of emotions with feelings oscillating between happiness and sadness. It was not the obituary that caused the upset because the feelings were already there: the obituary was simply the trigger to ill defined emotions that had been mine for several days beforehand.

Thus began what was to prove to be a very bewildering day with strong and mixed emotions. On one hand there was gratitude for a span of life that I never imagined possible eighteen months ago and on the other an acute awareness of the temporary nature of this respite. Along with this latter awareness was an eagerness to meet the process of dying. I realise that the latter sentiment may puzzle and possibly annoy one or two people because it seems so very negative and life denying. I love life and love this period of graced life that has been given to me but I am also anxious to meet my fate. My condition, baring a total remission, cannot but be terminal and so I realise that there is something fearful that awaits me further down the course of my life. I am sure that I will be able to face and deal with death given sufficient strength and support from friends and medical staff but this time of waiting generates a degree of apprehensiveness.

A few years ago I used to love to run in long distance road races. Though I say it myself, I was quite an accomplished runner and always in the top twenty per cent of any field. No matter how often I took part in races I always used to find the wait for the starting gun to go off the most difficult part of the race. During that time all the self doubt I had over my performance would come flooding into consciousness; had I prepared well enough; had I over trained and become too tired; were the laces on my shoes too tight or too slack; was the slight discomfort I felt in my shin going to prevent me from completing the course, etc.

Though I was with thousands of other runners I always had a great sense of aloneness realising that everything was down to me, no one could run the race for me. These were anxious moments and moments that I always dreaded; dreaded more than the pain and difficulty of competing in a long race. However, after the starting pistol had been fired all the anxiety faded away, the nervous energy went into my legs and away I went! I was then able to let go of my fantasies about the race, my fitness and problems I might have during the race. All I had to do was get round the course as fast as I could. On each and every occasion I took part in a race I discovered that this anticipatory period of fantasy prior to the race was always more of a problem than the actual race. This discovery taught me a valuable lesson in life that when we face a demanding or possibly painful situation the anticipation of it tends to be more difficult than the actual situation itself.

At the moment in this the "limbo" of my present life I can see a similitude between pre-race anxiety and my present state of health. When I hear that my cancer has once again started to grow a small part of me will, despite my love of life, be glad that it is now time to face what I fear. The power of human imagination is such that reality is seldom as awful as the imagined scenario. I do not fear death but I do fear the process of dying with its loss of independence and discomfort but I also know, through my running, that it is my fear and self doubt that have the greatest capacity to disable me. Reality, no matter how difficult, is always our friend and the more we are grounded in our own reality the safer we are; it is all too easy for us human beings to get lost in the "what ifs". My practice of meditation, like my running, has over a number of years helped me to cope better with fantasy and root myself ever deeper in reality. Reality is always our friend but major life events have the capacity to detach us from our rootedness and strengthen fantasy. Intuitively I knew that this might happen to me on this particular birthday and sure enough what I thought would happen did!

Perhaps the road race analogy has been triggered off by my clearing out some of the clothes in my wardrobe for among the items I cleared out was a pair of training shoes and a shoe bag. When I was running I used to only wear my running shoes for running and the shoe bag was used to carry my shoes to the races I used to take part in. It was easy to put them into the sack for their journey to the charity shop but in the early hours of the following morning the significance of my actions became more important. Once again there was a demand to let go of the past and embrace the new reality of my present state of health instead of remembering how I used to be. As I look around my room there are many more things that I know I will need to let go of as time passes but as yet the time has not come. The business of "letting go" is a process of invitation and response where one has to trust oneself to know when it is appropriate to let go of something, someone or even life itself. To do something before it is time to do it is to behave inappropriately and also hurt oneself; in these matters it is always better to trust the Process of life.

I owe a great debt to running for in that discipline I learned much about the life of the spirit. First of all I learned how foolish it is to try and grab the things that can only be given as a grace, a gift. When I first started running my ego would try and grasp fitness instead of recognising that what I desired in terms of performance could only be had as a "gift". The result was that for several months I kept injuring myself! There is nothing like pain for teaching wisdom and bringing about change. Eventually I learned to be content with my limitations whilst gently challenging myself to go ever further in speed and distance. Doing this enabled me to accept fitness as a gift whilst challenging me to become more accomplished than I previously was. One of the major lessons I learned through racing was not to be over concerned with how others were running their race; not to draw comparisons but be concerned about my own performance and run as good a race as I was capable of. At the end of a race I was always happy if I had run at the pace I knew I was capable of: this was proof positive I had run the race to the best of my physical and mental capability.

The lessons one learns in one aspect of life have the power to teach one invaluable lessons in other areas of life and so it was with me. The lessons I learned through long distance running taught me much about the life of the spirit. It taught me the need for a sprit of gentleness rather than competition, the foolishness of comparison with others and the need for personal discipline to be accomplished in anything. It was through the wisdom of my body that I learned to receive a new identity, one based not on what I can achieve but am prepared to receive by simply being attentive to the sacramentality of all life, even running!

Recently I have put together what I have called, "An Idiots Guide to Spiritual Development". It is a collection of thoughts about spiritual development for those people who are not very spiritually accomplished and for whom the "greats" of the spiritual life don't seem to answer the kind of questions they have. It is written primarily for those who have an interest in meditation but may be of interest to others. If you would like a copy of this please let me know and I will send it to you by e-mail.

Please keep me in your hearts as I keep you in mine.

My Dear Friends,

On the 14th of December I once again went to the hospital to see my oncologist who every two months monitors my condition. As I thought, my condition remains stable which, given my initial prediction of life expectancy, is a miracle in itself. As you will appreciate, this news is quite the best Christmas present I could have had. The hospital has monitored my condition from the time of my initial diagnosis and maintained a watching brief on the cancer ready to deal with symptoms as and when they arise; for this I am grateful. I remain free from discomfort and though I have a degree of breathlessness it is not a great handicap to me providing I live within the limitations of my condition. As I said in my last letter tiredness is my main symptom though one can never be too sure if the tiredness is part of the symptomatology or simple indolence!

As I am sure you have noticed Christmas fast approaches and with it all the pressures that last year one vowed one would never endure again. Sadly the season of Advent becomes overlooked in the feverish activity that accompanies Christmas preparation. I noticed in the "Scotsman", a Scottish daily newspaper, an article that reported the first Christmas tree of the year had been erected here in Scotland over six weeks before Christmas! Whether we like it or not we are "bounced" into the celebration of Christmas earlier and earlier without a time of preparation for the feast. In part this has to do with us becoming a more secular society.

Last year one person I know went into a shop in Dundee to buy Christmas cards and not seeing any religious cards asked an assistant if they had any other cards. The assistant said that they did have some "farmyard cards" if he would like to see them. Such a statement surely brings into stark focus the fact that we are living in a post Christian era. Christmas has tended to become a feast of consumerism and over indulgence and has lost touch with the Christian origins of the feast. At this point it would be very easy to get into "grumpy old man mode"; a tendency that I fear comes to me all too easily these days! However, I will resist the temptation and write about something that is precious to me, and all too regularly overlooked, the season of Advent.

The word Advent means arrival or coming of an important person but are we excited as we anticipate the future? I don't think so. If there is anything our world needs more than ever it is a sense of hope. Sadly we live in a world of cynicism whereby the very worst interpretation of a nation or persons actions are deemed to be the truth. In such a world "hope" has become a sorry joke and the search for God's entry into our world a futile exercise.

How easy it is on picking up a newspaper to become despairing of situations or people and miss the Potential that is being born in history. Having little or no hope we do not expect to see the latent possibilities in life and because we do not expect to see them we miss them. However, Advent is a time to try and reclaim hope by reconnecting us to the source of a hope that is forever struggling to be born in our world.

The uniting or gathering principle in our world seems to be the tribalism of mutual hatred and antipathy rather than the person of Christ. It is in the hearing of the "cock crow" of conscience, like Peter, or hearing the voice of expanded consciousness on the road to Damascus, like Paul, that we escape the cyclic repetitiveness that holds us prisoner.

However, we need to recognise the resistance we have to hearing these voices preferring instead to listen to the siren voice that looks to blame, accuse and condemn others. Thus it is that we continue to have the same failings in charity over and over again uniting with others in the "blame game" whilst never seeing ourselves as part of the problem.

A good number of years ago I remember listening to a recording of "Silent Night" as sung by Simon and Garfunkel. Whilst they were singing in beautiful harmony this most popular of Christmas carols, in the background, a radio was broadcasting the six o'clock news from New York. The two singers were singing of a holy night when "all was calm all was bright" whilst the radio was informing listeners of murders, assaults, rapes and scandals. The contrast could not have been starker and one was made very much aware that whilst Christ had come to bring hope to fallen humanity in a sense he had not fully achieved his mission.

One of the things that we should have inherited from the Jewish faith is a Messianic expectancy that leads us to look towards a golden age in the future. An Advent spirit is a spirit that looks for Something hidden in life's events be they joyful or painful. Looking for the coming of God in our world is an attempt to re-claim hope and the way to do that is to re-connect us to the religious heart of our faith, the incarnation. The incarnation of Christ, the intimate and inseparable link of human and divine, is a remedy for sin; the illusion that humankind can ever be separate from God and live an autonomous existence. In the birth of Christ God broke into history thus shattering the illusion of autonomy.

For us to be an Advent people it is necessary that we be conscious of the need of a "second coming" or to use a more precise word, Parousia; a word that means being fully present. At Christmas people generally celebrate Christ's coming in a limited way: limited in terms of place, Palestine; limited chronologically, the first century; limited to the lives of his followers. To be in Advent one has to feel that Something is happening in history, despite all pressures to believe the contrary, and the Parousia is now (Jn5:24).

Christ is to be born in the stable of our lives and the world situation in which we find ourselves. He was and is to be born in the most unlikely of places, at a time when no one expects and a time when darkness is at its deepest and most over powering. He will not, as the Wise Men of the infancy narrative found out, be born in the "palaces" of apparent order and piety where we might expect him to be born but in the mess and straw of who and how we and our world is at this present moment. That is why I found the recording of Simon and Garfunkel's "Silent Night" so memorable for it is into the mess and sordidness of human existence that the Christ child needs to come and does come, abolishing the distinction between the sacred and the profane.

At Christmas we celebrate that a new gathering principle is born into our world; the world of tribalism, discord and enmity. All of these are to be transcended; transcended in a person, the Person of Christ. Angelus Silesius expressed it in these terms, "If in your heart you make a manger for his birth, then God will once again become a child on earth". For the birth of the Divine to take place within us it is, as I said above, essential for us to listen to the cock crow of conscience and the voice of expanded consciousness on the road to Damascus.

As in the Simon and Garfunkle rendition of Silent Night there will be other voices in the background to distract us from what should be the focus of our attention. However, it is important to concentrate on the Singer and the Song rather than on the folly, sin and limitedness of human nature as reported in the news broadcast.

I will not be sending out cards this year but be assured that each and every one of you is remembered at this special time of year and held firmly in my heart. May you and yours have a Joyful, Blessed and Hope filled Christmas and New Year.

My Dear Friends,

It seems to me that life is composed of both "important" and "significant" events. What I mean by this is that it possible for an event to be significant in someone's life whilst seeming of little importance in the world's eyes.

An example of this for me was the decision by the Voluntary Euthanasia Societies to change its name to "Dignity in Dying": in the eyes of the world an unimportant event but in my life a highly significant event. I say this because implicit in the name change is the belief that only through euthanasia can one die with dignity. I happen to believe that this in not the case and my interest, given my health situation, is rather more than academic. The news of the proposed name change was given wide publicity on the radio and in the press. This happened at a time when the media were also giving a great deal of publicity to the case of Dr. Anne Turner who, with the aid of the Swiss organisation "Dignitas", terminated her own life. The heart rending statements of Dr Turner, a woman suffering from a slow and debilitating illness, about why she wished to terminate her life were given much prominence in the media. It was also about this time that Lord Joel Joffe - a retired human rights lawyer who defended Nelson Mandela – declared that he wanted the right to assisted suicide enshrined on the statute book.

Though these events are not as important as say the Iraq war they are highly "significant" and the fact that they all happened at approximately the same time is enough to arouse a degree of suspicion about the subtle promotion of assisted suicide. Is it only my presentiment that persons unknown, by means of a drip feed of selected information, aspire to change the pattern of terminal care in the U.K.? It could of course be that I am unduly sensitive to this kind of news release and thus prone to paranoiac ruminations. However, I don't actually believe this to be true but if this actually is a delusion then I wouldn't would I!

It would be both foolish and judgemental to comment upon the decision taken by Anne Turner to terminate her own life. When my present condition deteriorates to the extent that life becomes difficult, I too may hear the siren voice of "reason" advocating an early release. However, should this temptation occur, I will resist it not only for the customary reason that one's life is in the hands of God and one should await the call of the Divine, but because I believe that there is value in the process of dying. If one is in great pain or distress this may be difficult to believe but believe it we must along with employing every means possible to improve the quality of life available. Palliative care specialists, of whom there are too few, insist that there is no need for a person to die in severe pain given the knowledge we now have of pain relief. Whilst it is legitimate to give high doses of drugs to relieve pain, which have as a side effect the shortening of life, it does not seem to me appropriate to give drugs with the principle aim of destroying human life.

Evidence suggests that assisted suicide actually works against the establishment of good palliative care: the kind of care that permits a persons life to end rather than be broken off by an act of will. Supporters of assisted suicide would have it that it would be possible to legalise the termination of one's own life without there being consequences to those who would wish to choose another way of letting go of life. Whilst this sounds a more than reasonable argument in practice this is not true. Nowhere in the world where assisted suicide been legalised has the quality of palliative care increased in its availability or quality.

In the state of Oregon where assisted suicide has been legal for the last seven years it is possible for a person to have federal and state "healthcare" for assisted suicide. However, not all the treatments that would enable a better quality of life for the patient are similarly funded by the state or the government! Perhaps here we are beginning to see the more shadowy side of what is often presented as a humanitarian gesture towards those suffering a terminal condition.

In Holland assisted suicide has been legal for the last thirty years and here the situation is worse than it is in Oregon. As I understand it, in Holland one's condition does not even have to be terminal, one simply has to be suffering "unacceptable pain", a pain that may or may not be physical. With the advent of assisted suicide there has been a marked deterioration in research into pain relief and palliative care is less available. Along with this there is less attempt to teach general practitioners what pain relief is available to their terminally ill patients. Here surely is the evidence that assisted suicide actually destroys the kind of services we should be aspiring to. What was introduced into society as a "last resort" can and does all too easily become the "first resort" when faced with the deteriorating services brought about by the legalisation of assisted suicide.

I know from my own experience when one receives a diagnosis of a terminal condition one may well have overwhelming fears about what the future holds for one. What should happen is that one's questions need to be answered and one's fears about pain and discomfort need to be addressed. If this is not done the fear of pain, discomfort and the dread of being a burden upon those one loves might drive one to seek the termination of ones own life.

What seems like a humane gesture to save a person from human suffering can and does have implications for society as I have shown. Whilst not wishing to impose my own moral position upon others I am convinced of the need to help people such as myself who have a terminal condition live lives in as pain free and fulfilling a way as possible. Death is part of life and it is important to see it as such rather than a failure of medical science.

Watching the life of a person one loves slowly ebb away is always difficult and even more difficult if there is discomfort or distress in the beloved. What is happening seems senseless to us and one hopes for a speedy release of suffering, for the suffering seems to have no purpose to it. However, because the anguish does not seem to make sense does not mean that there cannot be a "gift" in it, no matter how deeply it may be "buried". What is required of us is to suspend our judgement and be less sure of what should happen and how things should be. This was a very valuable lesson I learned from the last illness and death of my mother.

My mother died of arteriosclerotic dementia and over the course of several years the person that my sister and I knew was lost to us in what was a protracted bereavement. Over the years her speech became increasingly confused and she employed many neologisms; so much so that it was totally impossible to understand what she was saying. One day as I was sitting holding her hand, for that was all one could do when visiting, she said, "My mother was very strict with me and it doesn't always do". After saying this she once again drifted on into the customary word salad of her confused speech. In that moment I realised that one can never guess what is taking place in another and what it is that they might be "working through".

Human life is a kind of story that needs pondering, organising and possibly re-telling to oneself. If you are a person of faith it is a story that one needs to be open to the loving mercy of God in its re-telling. It is a time to accept the waning of ones powers and the finite nature of our belonging upon the face of the earth. Early foreclosure on life can mean the lack of opportunity for this work of what we used to call "soul making".

It is also easy to overlook the grace, the gift, which the dying person can be for those about them. For example, my mother was a woman of her time and therefore not an emotionally demonstrative person. As mother's dementia increased her inhibitions fell away and she became the most loving person I have ever encountered. All my life I had questioned whether I was loved, whether I was wanted as a child. During the final years of her life the doubts were washed away by the unbounded depths of her love. But this love was not just for me as all the persons who attended her when she was struggling to live an independent life in her home and those who looked after her in the final stages of her illness spoke of her in the same manner. Had mother terminated her own life at the onset of her illness to prevent her condition from becoming "degrading" it would have robbed me of the greatest gift God has ever given me and robbed those around her of an instrument of God's love.

Sadly we do not live in a society that values age and infirmity but a society that worships the cults of youth, consumerism, and efficiency; a culture that sees the process of death as a "failure" rather than part of life. The task of re-appraising the story of one's life and living through the process of dying is no longer seen for being what it is, a creative act and one of the most precious things that one can do. The fact that one wants to speed either oneself or another through this process is a sure indicator of how alienated we as a society have become from the process of life; a process that includes both living and dying. Whilst reading a few articles on this subject I came across a quote from Cicely Saunders, the founder of the hospice movement, who said that a good death was one where, "as the body becomes weaker so the spirit becomes stronger".

In a few months time it will be two years since I was diagnosed with a terminal condition and given between six and twelve months to live. Had I decided on hearing of my condition to have ended my life I would have robbed myself of the most productive, insightful and fecund period of my life. In a spiritually sensitive culture this would unquestionably be believed but so alienated from the Truth have we become that it needs to be recalled to people's memory. I hope that this brief letter has served to at least keep before your eyes issues which you know in your heart to be true.

I am sure that you will be pleased to know that my health still remains stable and, insofar as I can, I keep busy with duties appertaining to my Order and to the asbestos charity I am connected with. On the twenty seventh of this month, Mesothelioma Day, I am to attend a conference in Clydebank on asbestos related diseases. Clydebank has a very high number of mesothelioma victims, owing to it being the centre of shipbuilding on the Clyde, and it is intended to have a national memorial to those who have died from this disease outside what was John Browns shipyard. It is ironic that the factory that I worked at provided the asbestos later to be sprayed on the bulkheads of ships built in the Clydebank yards; asbestos that was later to be responsible for the deaths of so many in that town.

Please continue to keep me in your prayers along with all the people who work to bring support and comfort to those suffering from asbestos related diseases.

My Dear Friends,

First of all the good news that on a recent hospital visit to see my oncologist I was told what I already knew in my bones that my condition remains stable. As you will appreciate, this is as good a piece of news as is possible for me to have in the circumstances in which I find myself.

Many thanks to those of you who kindly followed through on my request to support the Mesothelioma Charter organised by the British Lung Foundation. I would also like to extend a special word of thanks to those of you who spontaneously recruited friends and work colleagues to follow your example and support the Charter. I am pleased to say that the Charter received great support and one would hope that the government and political parties would pay heed to what is being asked.

Feeling fairly well I have been able to travel and the last week has seen me in Belfast and Clydebank. Clydebank, just outside Glasgow, was the centre of shipbuilding on the Clyde and has the dubious privilege of being the mesothelioma capital of the United Kingdom. On the twenty seventh of February, Mesothelioma Day, an organisation called Clydebank Asbestos Group organised a conference on mesothelioma.

The event had speakers from South Africa, Canada and all parts of the United Kingdom, all of whom had specialist knowledge. The speakers came from the world of politics, trade unionism, the medical profession, the legal profession or had expert knowledge due to their activism in asbestos related issues. The conference attracted some three hundred participants, principally from Scotland but many from other parts of the U.K. Some participants were members of various interest groups and professions whilst others had a direct connection with asbestos related disease.

I found the day stimulating, enlightening and very tiring for though my energy level is quite good at the moment the schedule of the conference I found to be punishing. I met some very fine people at the conference and was able to put faces to names. The conference also gave me the opportunity to meet people I had not seen for a while and thus provided the chance for an exchange of news. A few days before the conference Clydebank Asbestos Group asked if I would be prepared to give interviews to the media but, after reflection, decided against this. I decided not to do this because I did not want to draw attention to myself and my condition, living as I do in a very small town. However, I was pleased to think that others had sufficient confidence in me as to believe that first of all I had something to say and secondly the ability to convey it in a reasonably articulate way. After the conference it occurred to me that I look so well at the moment that no one would believe that there was anything wrong with me so perhaps its would not have been a good idea to appear before the television cameras!

When I returned home friends asked me if I had enjoyed the conference to which I replied, "No, but it was both interesting and disturbing". If one were to have asked those leaving the hall how they felt at the end of the day I am sure they would have spoken about how well the conference was organised and said that it a very good experience. I too would have said the same things but when I got into my car my eyes filled with tears. I was unable to understand what the tears were about initially but during the night I woke up feeling angry and disturbed.

As you will appreciate, the subject of the conference was itself emotive and some of the topics, such as the palliative care of the mesothelioma patient, were not always easy for me to listen to. However, I think that what disturbed me most about the conference was the way that some of the speakers seemed to imply that there were "goodies" and "baddies" in the asbestos cause: a world in which reality is split into two parts, good and evil.

In such a dualistic world view "salvation" depends upon identifying oneself wholly with the "good guys" and projecting all one's evil on the "bad guys". The theologian Paul Tillich once commented that "the weakness of the fanatic is that those whom he fights have a secret hold upon him" (The Courage to Be). When we project all our "evil" upon another we create a relationship of dependence; that is we are dependent upon them as enemies to carry all the things in ourselves we do not want to see. If we don't have an enemy we must invent one. For example, with the end of the Cold War we had no "enemy" so we had to invent one and so we now speak of not the Cold War but the War of Terror. If we did not have an enemy to unite against how could we possibly justify our expenditure on militarism and arms – we are therefore dependent upon having an enemy.

As a child I remember going to the Saturday afternoon cinema for children where we would watch a variety of super heroes vanquishing the "bad guy". In such films one is provided with a scapegoat on whom one can externalise the evil side of one's own personality and in the disowning of it one never comes to any insight or awareness of its presence within oneself.

However, such super heroes and cartoon characters are not like us ordinary mortals – they have no "shadow side" and it is because they have no shadow they are not real. You would never get such a super hero telling lies to cover up their mistakes nor do they receive money for doing their good deeds. Similarly they never take advantage of the damsel they rescue and always act from the very best of motives. The anti-hero on the other hand is never redeemed, can never apologise or see the error of his ways and lead a changed life; instead he is destroyed or condemned to live on the fringe of society where he can do no more harm.

But real life is not like this and all of us need to put the infantile morality of the comic book hero behind us and root ourselves a little more firmly in reality. In order for us to be real it is essential that we recognise that we like every living and breathing person have a shadow side. Being adult involves us accepting that we and the institutions we belong to are less than perfect and realise that this is a common condition, a condition that we share with the rest of humanity. Failure to recognise this means that we don't take responsibility for our own shadow side and so we are inclined to project upon others all our failings and less than noble actions.

I found it strange that many of those who spoke, both from the platform and the floor, insisted that employers knew many years ago of asbestos related illnesses and kept this information to themselves. Can it really be true that for nearly a century, as some people claim, only the employers knew of the ill effects of asbestos? If this statement really was true then this must have been the best kept secret the world has ever known. Are we really to believe that the politicians of the left and union leaders were so out of touch with health and safety issues that they did not know information which they also claim had been known for nearly a century by employers?

If it is true that the sinister effects of asbestos were known so long ago why did these politicians and unions do nothing about protecting workers from it? They had a duty of care and, as I see it, they failed in that duty if, as suggested, research had been done in this area and they knew nothing about it. However, like super heroes and unlike the villainous employers they believe they have nothing to apologise for. I do not know when the dangers of asbestos were known because so many people make different claims. But if unions and politicians postulate a theory that such knowledge had been available for many years they also have to produce a sensible argument as to why they or their advisors could have been so ill informed of the health risks to their members. Perhaps some smart lawyer will one day decide to sue the unions for failure to protect their membership!

Similarly the lawyers spoke as if they too had nothing that they had no issues to address. However, you will not be too surprised to hear that I think they have. Several months ago I read an article that was sent to me by a friend in Canada. The article stated that there were groups of personal injury lawyers in the States soliciting spurious claims for damages arising from asbestos related disease. To further their aims they had employed mobile x-ray vans to tour the country and these, together with the services of a radiologist who was prepared to diagnose mesothelioma on the strength of one x-ray, produced a large number of claims against asbestos companies. The article went on to explain that owing to the number of these somewhat suspect claims companies were choosing to go into Chapter 11 bankruptcy. I have no way of knowing how true the claims in this article are but the claims seem to be borne out in an article in the Newyorker which can be viewed at:- http://www.newyorker.com/talk/content/?060306ta_talk_surowiecki If there is any truth at all in these articles the legal profession needs to rid itself of these ambulance chasers and legal pirates.

In my civil claim against Federal Mogul, the American company that took over the firm I worked for, I believe that I will be awarded the princely sum of seventeen pence in the pound in my claim for damages against that company. However, the lawyers representing my case will no doubt receive payment in full for their representation of my case. And where will the money come from? Well, I guess that it will come from funds that might have been used as compensation for people like me whose lives have been brought to a premature end. Personal injury lawyers in the U.K. are doing so well out of these asbestos claims that some of them are able to support the work of asbestos charities and their workers. They look upon the support of these agencies as a way of getting referrals and generating income for their firm.

It often happens that the institutions we have created tend to "have" us; they take over our lives. We become slaves to the "worldly spirituality" of the institution without us realizing what has happened. This leads us to behave in ways that deny the truth of the mistakes we have made, the damage we have done and the consequences of that damage to others; all that matters is the survival of the company or institution.

Without institutions, ideas can't move into action and organisations do have to have concern for their own structures but these needs must always be penultimate never ultimate. It is a very sad fact that most institutions place their own good above the general welfare of others. For example, a company may try and cut corners on costs and produce a defective product that my lead to the injury of those who use that product. Union leadership can and often does become more preoccupied with extending its political aims and aspirations rather than defending the rights and safety of its members. All institutions be they factories, unions, parliaments or churches exist to serve values beyond themselves but the sad reality is that the primary purpose tends to get lost in the day to day running of an institution.

It is not my intention to have a rant at each and every group that are trying to achieve justice for those of us who suffer from asbestos related diseases but to ask them to acknowledge that they too are flawed people in a flawed institution and don't do everything well. Part of being human is the recognition that we don't always live from our best selves. Sometimes we make mistakes or act from cowardly motives. Without a realisation that we too are flawed we can make acts of civil disobedience, demonstrations, verbal confrontations, or even conference speeches rituals that are there to affirm our own "purity". Company loyalty, professional loyalty, comradely loyalty, are noble things but can blind us to the truth. When this happens the primary goal of the institution or professional body is forgotten and all that counts is the purity of the institution or organisation. This in turn means that all the "badness" is projected upon a scapegoat who is then compelled to carry a burden that rightly belongs to us individually and collectively.

The earliest teaching on projection in the New Testament is [Mat 7:3 -5] "Why do you see the splinter in your neighbour's eye, but do not notice the log in your own eye? Or how can you say to your neighbour, 'Let me take the speck out of your eye,' while the log is in your own eye? You hypocrite, first take the log out of your own eye, and then you will see clearly to take the speck out of your neighbour's eye".

The splinter in your neighbour's eye is perhaps a chip off the log in your own and the reason that Jesus suggests there is a log in our own eye has to do with the log in my eye totally blinding me! If I remove that which blinds me then I am in a position to help my neighbour to remove the splinter from their own eye. In our blindness we are prevented from loving our enemies because we need them as targets for our projections. By discharging our hatred upon external enemies, we can achieve a partial release of pent up energy that is festering in our unconscious but we can never change ourselves.

One of the speakers at the conference, a politician, told the story of meeting Nelson Mandela in Northern Ireland where he was trying to promote the peace process. The speaker said that Mandela told the politicians of the North that the thing they needed to do was to change themselves, for only in changing themselves would the political situation in Ireland change. This passing remark was the most important contribution to the day for me. Like the Northern Ireland politicians many at the conference were too sure as who the good guys were and who the bad guys were. I am not so sure that any group is wholly good and certain that no one is wholly bad. I am also sure that every person is redeemable; that is they can change if given opportunity to do so.

The Church does not exist to serve the world but to preach to it by the living out of values that challenge a "worldly spirituality". It is not enough to simply look after the worlds casualties but to bring about a new world order in which every man and woman is one's brother and sister. Jesus tells us to love our enemies and that is why the true Christian should never be quite at home in this world because they have a bigger world view than their compatriots.

The problems that we face as humans can never be overcome by one sector of society lashing out at another. At root our problems are common and the solution of them needs to be common. The powers of destruction are within us all and all of us need to "come home" to whom and how we are rather than project upon others elements of personality we find difficult to cope with.

The Prophets of the Old Testament equated the abuse of others with a turning away from God. The prophet Amos stated that it was because people turned away from God that they did terrible things to each other. But we must continually be on our guard against bogus religion and ersatz interiority whose sole purpose is that of evasion. A spiritual life that is only concerned with achieving heaven or "enlightenment" is a spirituality that can be contained in any culture or economic system.

The spiritual attack upon Nazism came from people like Bonhoeffer, who were people of deep prayer, people who took up a critical attitude towards the false gods of their time. If you cannot see the truth in a situation your actions will always be flawed, for action should always flow from vision. The famous activist against the Vietnam war, Fr. Dan Berrigan wrote these words on the need for deep prayer:-

"The time will shortly be upon us, if it is not already here, when the pursuit of contemplation becomes a strictly subversive activity... I am convinced that contemplation, including the common worship of the believing, is a political act of the highest value, implying the riskiest of consequences to those taking part."

This is so because the contemplative is the one who confronts the world of false consciousness and can see the systems that are a product of this false consciousness. That is because he or she is rooted in a Unity that transcends all the manmade divisions we are inclined to take for reality. I think that this concept is beautifully described by the contemplative and social activist Fr. Richard Rohr in these words:-

"To pray is to build your own house. To pray is to discover that Someone else is within your house. To pray is to recognise that it is not your house at all. To keep praying is to have no house to protect because there is only One House. And that One House is everybody's Home... That is the politics of prayer. And that is probably why truly spiritual people are always a threat to politicians of any sort. They want our allegiance and we can no longer give it. Our house is too big."

When one catches a glimpse of the Oneness of creation, albeit briefly, one knows the only truth that is worth having. From then on there can be no "enemies" for all are one in Christ. However, from time to time one may well slip back into an earlier mode of existence and get locked into the world of opposites but this will be for a short time only. Having known the Unity of all things one never forgets this foundational experience and after a while proper vision is restored.

When one is in a setting where everyone is presenting unreality as reality it becomes very disturbing because there is a conflict between external "reality" and the experience of the Real. At such times one can be almost overcome by the resulting disturbance but in the quiet of one's own heart vision is restored and one can see the spiritual famine and loss of vision that are so much a part of our Western world, prone as it is to fanaticism in its myriad forms.

Some would have it that prayer is a substitute for action whereby we push onto God the responsibility for doing what God is empowering us to do in his name. The sad truth is that we have become so alienated from authentic spiritual values that we have for the most part lost the ability as Christians to live prophetic lives. To be a "prophet" is to be a seer rather than a thinker or listener of the Word.

Proper perception can't be brought about by reading books, listening to lectures but by a simple openness to the Truth. As E.M. Forster once said, "Only what is seen sideways sinks deep". The perception which we need can't be engineered but is something that creeps up on us with cat-like stealth. This lack of sight is the crisis of our age and the only remedy I know is the practice of the prayer of silence. Some would have it that prayer is a substitute for action whereby we push onto God the responsibility for doing what God is empowering us to do in his name. True prayer is not and never should be seen as an escape from the common lot of humanity but as a sharing in the redemption of the world and of common life.

Perhaps we could say that the Christian is one who should take up a critical stance towards the world and its structures. During this season of the Churches year, Lent, maybe we could learn to fast from quick and easy judgement of people and situations and be prepared to search for the goodness in each and every person.

Please keep in your heart a friend of mine who died from cancer a few days ago Sr. Brigid McEvoy. Brigid would be well known to those of you who have been involved in Christian Meditation in the West of Scotland were she ran the Paisley meditation group for a good number of years. She worked for most of her religious life with the deaf in Newcastle and Glasgow and will be remembered by all who came into contact with her for her signing ability which one person once described to me as being "poetic". Her funeral Mass is to take place on Monday the 6th of March in Newcastle.

My Dear Friends,

Easter comes round once again and with it the reassurance that goodness will, in the end, always overcome hatred and wrongdoing. In the person of Christ hanging on the cross we see both the selfless potential for "giving" in human nature and also what human nature has it in its power to do to goodness.

I have searched in vain for a Holy Week or Easter theme within myself but failed to find the necessary inspiration. As you know these letters are written as and when things "touch" me. Much has been happening in my life but these events seem almost too trivial to write about as separate entities and so I was prompted to reflect on whether there had been a recurrent theme.

Over the last few weeks I feel I have been involved in making decisions about present realities or weighing up how to make decisions that will affect the future treatment of my cancer. Some of these decisions have been reached after much self searching, personal pain and difficulty and this has led me to reflect upon how and why I have made the decisions that I have.

Making decisions is never easy especially when one knows that whatever decisions one arrives at will affect others and possibly hurt people who one loves and admires. I think that my basic rule in decision making is to assume that one is doing the right thing until one knows one isn't! This may seem a trite and possibly trivial thing to say but I believe it is necessary to remind myself of this from time to time as it generally prevents me from getting lost in the "what if's"

As I reflect upon the major decisions of my life I can see that most if not all of them have been decisions that have, as it were, made themselves. By saying this I do not mean that I have simply drifted along in a blind and unreflective way, but they have been made as a result of simply holding in my heart everything appertaining to the decision making process until a course of action "emerged".

This process requires that one does not make a decision before one is ready or able to do so, for it is essential that the decision made be in accord with the depths of one's being. I have written before about Christ being in the Garden of Gethsemane and the possibility he had of fleeing his captors by walking away into the wilderness. Sometimes just staying with a situation of conflict or tension until we know in the depths of our being what we have to do is the height of bravery.

The temptation is always one of making our decisions from the wrong "place" within us and thus it becomes possible to do what may be the "right" thing for the "wrong reason". What I am trying to say is that unless our decisions come from the integration of our actions with the ultimate Source of life we run the risk of harming others. This problem of "right action" is a very real and a very deep one for contemporary men and women, stemming as it does from our deepest identity and our security in that identity.

In most if not all of us there is a dislocation between the "surface self" that is lost upon the sea of illusion and self-deception and the "inner self"; that is why it is so hard for us to make decisions. Decision making and action can't simply be worked out from some idea or precept given to us by an individual or a society that, like us, is "born out of true".

Thomas Merton in his book "Seeds of Contemplation" writes the following:-

"Identity is not merely to have a face and a name, a recognisable physical presence. Identity in this deep sense is something that one must create for himself by choices that are significant and that require a courageous commitment in the face of anguish and risk. This means much more than having an address and a name in the telephone book. It means having a belief one stands by; it means having certain definite ways of responding to life, of meeting its demands, of loving other people, and in the last analysis of serving God. In this sense, identity is one's witness to truth in one's life".

So according to Merton right action is really the problem of who we are: the principles we act on, how we choose these principles and who I am before God. In short there needs to be a shift of attention from action to attention. This shift of focus will not come about easily but needs to be worked upon. If we are to be fully human and able to act as such, then we need more than "willing" or "choosing"; we need to learn to pay attention and live our lives from the sacred place within ourselves. All too often we live on the surface of life trying to live our lives by means of the rational will and other people's rules, wishes or principles rather than living out of our own Reality.

By simply having a patient loving regard towards a person, task or situation we build up a true impression of "what is", what the world really is like. This happens not simply at the point of decision but a long time before then. When the received information is in accord with the depths of our being we will act but we can only act when we can act and not a moment before. In this way we make decisions in obedience to who we are and how we understand things. Because the decision is made from a place within ourselves where we are at "One" with others our decision can't be rooted in pride or egocentricity: the needs of others will be as important as those of our own

The enemy of right action is fantasy and self-aggrandisement both of which prevent us from seeing what is. We need to be set free from this fantasy world and world of self seeking if we are to act properly and morally. In other words we have to learn to practice detachment, a word that these days is little understood or valued.

Detachment is a process by which we learn to direct our attention outward, away from the superficial self that tends to cling and grasp at people, things and power. Freedom is often thought of as the simple exercise of the will but nothing could be further from the truth. True freedom is rooted in proper perception, accurate vision and living in obedience to our true nature.

The sad truth is that we are inclined to see things in the way we want to see them rather than looking at things the way they are. Our perception is inclined to be governed by our apparent needs, and so we live our lives not just on the surface of things but also, in some real way, apart from things as they are. We are dominated by the superficial self who seeks power, pleasure and possessions to build itself up. The realisation that we are not authentic people, un-spiritual people, and living as we do from what is superficial in us is the beginning of true wisdom.

To be a spiritual person is to live what has been given to us in its deepest possible dimensions. It is to live what we are in our depths and to know what we truly are is rooted in That of God within ourselves.

This dislocation between the superficial self, with its strategies for happiness, and the true or deeper self manifests itself in a kind of "materialism", a desire to accumulate things to itself.

This striving for more "things", power, prestige or possessions, is a symptom of our alienation from the deeper self that is in union with all other Self's, Creation and God. However, the desire to accrue money, status, job, power, etc is a flawed strategy to develop a sense of identity that is separate to and apart from the Divine Spark within us. The Church has traditionally referred to this condition as original sin.

Materialism is a symptom of our alienation or dislocation which causes us to want to appropriate things to ourselves but the things that we try to cling to are not necessarily concrete or physical. For example, it is possible for us to become over attached to positions, roles, power, religious tenets or spiritual experiences. In our spiritual search it is essential that we drive from the temple of our hearts the "merchant" who tries to amass spiritual riches and vainly tries to negotiate a "good deal" from God.

This kind of prideful clinging, along with the other kinds of attachments, are vain attempts to try and get life on our own terms and live our lives for ourselves. In short they are rooted in the egocentricity that is so much a part of unredeemed humanity. Sadly such a way of living cuts us off from a Unity we already have in the depths of our being; a unity with Others, Creation and God. But all we have to do to remedy the situation is to simply "come home" to who we are in our depths and live in humble obedience to That of God in us.

I began this letter by saying that I could not think of an Easter theme but as I write this brief missive I realise that what I have written could be seen as a prompt to the Gospel call to "die to self" and live to Christ; a theme very appropriate for this liturgical season. As I wrote the phrase, "die to self", the words seemed to be simplistic, trite and over used.
   However, despite the familiarity of these words there is a depth in them that we continually need to rediscover if our faith is to be a living faith rooted in life experience rather than dry concepts.

I am reminded of G. K. Chesterton's book Orthodoxy in which he writes of someone leaving a land that is familiar and setting out to sea. After sailing for a while one notices what seems to be an exotic pagan temple. Excited one rows towards it only to find out that it is the Brighton Pavilion! The longer I live the more I see the Gospel story as being an ever more relevant commentary on my life rather than a story of something that happened two thousand years ago. When one's life story links up with the Gospel teachings and this happens of itself a teaching that appeared to be "dead" through over use becomes resurrected and full of life.

This morning I went to the hospital for my usual two monthly check up and was told once again that my cancer still remains stable. There has been little change in my condition since August of last year and for this I am truly grateful. However, two weeks ago whilst visiting our London Priory I developed a tummy bug that led to my becoming dehydrated; so much so that a visit to hospital was necessary. The hospital staff were very kind to me and gave me an anti-emetic to stop me vomiting and intra-vinous fluids.

I had expected that I would recover from this without much of a problem but my underlying condition meant that it took nearly a fortnight before the bug was completely out of my system and my appetite returned. I must admit that this was a reminder to me that from now on it will always be more difficult to recover from conditions that once upon a time I would simply have shrugged off. This is a new reality to embrace and a reminder, if I needed one that whilst I am very well indeed there is still a "shadow" that hangs over my life.

As I look forward to the celebration of another Holy Week and Eastertide I thank God for the life given to me and thank him too for the gift of your support and friendship. May every Joy and Blessing be yours for this very special time of the year.

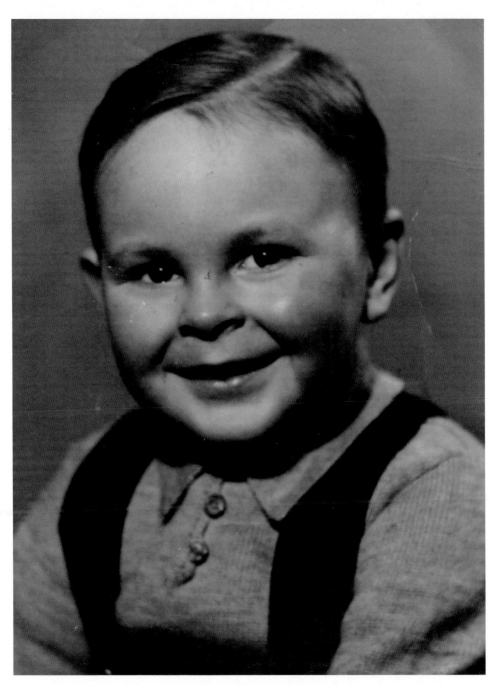

Early School Days

Peter on his first Holy Communion Day, St. Joseph's, Leigh

Peter takes Solemn Vows at Our Lady of Dolours, Servite Church, Fulham Road. 3rd July 1976

Peter being congratulated on his Solemn Profession by the Provinicial Peter Conniffe

Meditation Conference at St. Vincent's, Dundee

Peter acting as Chairman at the Provincial Chapter April 1994 with the Prior General Hubert Moons sitting next to him.

Peter studying at his desk in Mansionhouse Road, Glasgow.

Peter visiting his mother in the nursing home at Leigh shortly before her death in 1999

Peter with sculptor Janet Fox Pitt with the statue of St. Columba commissioned for the Servite Priory Benburb

Peter in his house at Tayport with his favourite Icon.

Peter vsiting the Isle of Iona in 2003

Peter with Margaret McBennet and Paul Harris on the beach at Broughty Ferry, September 2005

Peter with Margaret & Paul on the Isle of Lindisfarne, 2005

Peter celebrating his 60th birthday, November 2005 at Broughty Ferry with Alex Holmes, Graham, Margaret, Peter, Colm McGlynn and his sister Marie

A rose that Peter tended in his garden at Tayport

Looking across from Tayport to Broughty Ferry

My Dear Friends,

This morning I went to hospital to see my oncologist and heard the news that there has been some deterioration in my condition.

The cancer has spread further on my left lung and it would seem to have spread to my heart. The consequence of this further spread of the cancer seems to have led to the build up of fluid around my heart. However, this can only really be ascertained by means of a scan after which the situation will become clearer and a course of treatment more obvious. I have a further hospital appointment in five weeks and by that time the results of the scan should be available. I am told that my heart would seem to be fine and coping well with the extra burden placed upon it so there is no need to panic!

The change in my condition was not entirely unexpected. Over the last month I noticed that my breathing had become a little more difficult and this combined with unusual sensations in my chest, led me to believe that there had been a slight deterioration in my health. Given the slow development of my cancer the oncologist is recommending further chemotherapy with a new drug that has been developed specifically for the treatment of mesothelioma. However, it would be foolish to speculate about possible treatment options at this time because the full facts of what is happening within my chest wall are not known.

One thing I do know is that I have now lived twice as long as I was expected to! To say the least this has been a very strange experience for me. On one hand there is a delight at feeling as if I am cheating "nature" and on the other hand the feeling of being a charlatan for not having passed beyond the great divide when expected!

Two years ago I cancelled commitments that I had in hand expecting illness to prevent me from fulfilling the engagements made. However, apart from a brief spell of illness the expected bad health never arrived. As you will appreciate, I do have an underlying health problem and as a result do not have the energy I formerly had but am still able to engage with various activities and pursuits. I am careful not to overtax myself and all the commitments I undertake are undertaken on the understanding that whilst I will endeavour to fulfil the commitment it is possible that my health may prevent me from honouring the commitment.

In times past I would have travelled considerable distances giving talks on Christian Meditation and organising retreats and events connected with meditation. The last two years even with their restrictions have given me opportunity to do a variety of new things and learn to live in a new way. Before being ill my life was lived with an almost monastic rigour the day being punctuated by prayer at specific times which also necessitated strict times for rising and going to bed.

These days there is less rigidity in my lifestyle with my body determining how I live my life. If I feel tired at ten in the morning, even though I have only been up just over three hours, I will take a nap and do so without the guilt of former years. However, I think that it is also important to recognise that such a way of living is only possible if one has become reasonably self disciplined beforehand. In other words such a way of living is possible because there is some kind of inner framework to ones life due to a structured way of life. I suppose that what I am learning to do is to live my life through the wisdom of my body rather than the self imposed structures of former years. I would like to say that this is an achievement but can't do so because it is not some clever thing that I have done, it just happened of itself.

"Bodies" in Roman Catholic circles have often had a "bed press" but any spirituality that slights the needs of the body is not Christian. One of the questions in the old "Penny Catechism" was, "Of which must I take most care my body or my soul?" To which the answer was, "I must take most care of my soul because my soul is immortal". The following Sunday I would then go along to church and say the following during the recitation of the creed, "I believe in the resurrection of the body..". At the time I saw no contradiction in these two statements and, insofar as I am aware, neither did many others. Christians of a certain age, despite the incarnation with its obvious valuing of bodily life, are inclined to live in their heads. But why should this be the case? The truth of the matter is that the lingering feelings of we older generation must be seen for what they are elements of Jansenism that percolated into elements of our early religious training: as a consequence they should be ignored.

The truth of the matter is that a Christian needs to accept his or her bodiliness knowing that he or she can only go to God through his or her body and God can only come to them through their body. Despite the incarnation being a core belief of Christianity the Second Vatican Council felt it necessary to declare, "It is not permitted to despise the bodily life" (Gaudium et Spes Ch1:14). From the earliest times a false asceticism has tried to impose itself – an asceticism that is derived from a hatred of the body – a hatred born of fear and pride.

We need to remember that Jesus himself was criticised for not being ascetic enough (Mt 11:19). People could understand John the Baptist being "religious" because of his asceticism but not Jesus who enjoyed the good things of the world. However, Jesus refused to change and be what they wanted him to be – a kind of "Holy Willie" – and so they challenged him. When challenged he says, "The wedding guests cannot mourn as long as the bridegroom is with them, can they? The days will come when the bridegroom is taken away from them, and then they will fast." What Jesus is saying is that the fast of his followers will be his absence which will call for a fast of faith. It is the fast of faith that refuses to fill ourselves with the assurances our nature craves but reaches out in simple blind faith to a God that lies beyond the world of the senses. A proper Christian asceticism has its roots in love of God not in fear of the body.

The body has greater wisdom than the mind and tells us many things about ourselves and our needs. For example, it tells us when to eat and not eat, when to sleep and when to be attentive, when to talk and when to be silent. However, we are seldom gifted with sufficient body awareness to live our lives in the way that is appropriate. When we eat is all too often governed by time and need of "comfort" rather than bodily need. We live our lives tossed this way and that by imaginary "needs" of all kinds the only remedy for which is a deep prayer life that leads us from self- centeredness to other-centeredness.

Ones spiritual development one cannot bypass the body if one's spirituality is genuinely Christian because human nature in its origin is deiform – the divine life is within us. In an authentically Christian spirituality one enters into one's own being to the point where the human meets the Divine and in this meeting matter is transformed. Because of the union of two natures in Christ all humanity was called into communion with God in and through the flesh. The incarnation is therefore not only an event but a process and this is why a proper understanding of this great mystery is of supreme importance to us.

Looked at in this way the Ascension is not a solitary act where Jesus removes himself from us but a raising up of the human race into divine fellowship. St. Ambrose in commenting of the Ascension wrote, "It was not merely one man, but the whole world that entered" (heaven). St. Paul in his letter to the Ephesians (Eph 4:10) wrote, "Christ ascended beyond the heavens in order to fill the universe with his presence". The ascension is a vindication of Christ and the raising up or deification of humankind.

Without the truth of God being in Christ, the incarnation, the work of atonement and our participation in the life of God becomes meaningless: it all hinges on the incarnation.

When I start to write these letters I am never quite sure where they will take me and this letter is no exception to the rule. This is also the case with talks that I give for whilst I do prepare them quite meticulously with regard to both content and time, sometimes the content seems to have a life of its own. When this happens it is a very humbling experience.

With regard to talks, on Saturday the 26th of August at 11-00am I will be giving a talk in the Catholic Church, Our Lady Star of the Sea, Queen Street, Tayport. As in previous years there will be a talk followed by quiet prayer after which people will be welcome to visit my home for a light lunch. I do not need to know how many people will attend the talk but it is necessary to know how many people we need to cater for. So if you are able to attend the talk and wish to stay for lunch please contact Margaret McBennett, 158, St. Vincent Street, Broughty Ferry, Dundee DD5 2EX (01382 778375) mm010c1302@blueyonder.co.uk If you will let Margaret know numbers by Saturday the 19th of August this would enable her and her helpers to plan menus and quantities. As usual there will be something of a crush but it always is a wonderful experience to meet both old and new friends in an informal setting.

I will be taking a weeks holiday from Saturday the 24th of June and I look forward to visiting once again the delightful city of York, If you have not yet had your vacation may I wish you good weather and good company for your holiday; may your break be everything you would wish it to be.

My Dear Friends,

As some of you will know my condition took a severe dip after publication of my most recent letter saying that my cancer had developed further.

A week after the letters circulation I became very breathless; so much so that I had to cut short my holiday in York and return home to Tayport. Within just a few days of my return it became obvious to me that I needed an emergency appointment with my oncologist. I received an appointment a few days after requesting it and when I went to the hospital the consultant immediately arranged for my immediate admission to Ward 32 of Ninewells Hospital Dundee.

Within two hours of my admission the cause of the sudden breathlessness was ascertained by an echocardiogram confirming that fluid around my heart was restricting its beating. I was admitted to hospital at 11-30am on Thursday the 6th and all treatments and investigations took place on the same day! This afforded little time and opportunity to become anxious about the procedures necessary to remove what proved to be over half a litre of fluid.

The draining of the fluid around the heart took place in the Coronary Care Unit and was performed by a cardiologist who passed a needle, followed by a catheter, into the area where the depth of fluid was greatest. I was amazed that such a procedure is possible without stopping the heart and marvelled at the confidence shown by the cardiologist for whom this is an ordinary practice. I can't say that I found the procedure particularly pleasant but was pleased at the almost instantaneous relief of my breathing difficulties. After an overnight stay on the Coronary Care Unit where my condition was monitored via the very latest technology I returned to my bed on the Oncology Ward for a couple of hours before they decided I could return home.

Later this week I have a further echocardiogram to determine if the fluid is once again building up around my heart and as you can possibly imagine I am slightly apprehensive about the result. It is hoped that a course of chemotherapy might prevent further build up of fluid but the big question is whether or not these symptoms are just part of the management of a long term illness or mark a dramatic change in my condition. At the moment no one can say and it is time and time alone that will reveal that whether or not we are dealing with a dramatic change in my condition or simply a milestone in what is a long term chronic illness. As you will appreciate this "unknown-ness" is not always easy to deal with because I always like to know what it is that I am facing or dealing with.

Once again faith is what is required and given how well things go when I don't try to interfere one would expect faith to come easily but it doesn't. I take comfort from the response of the man whom Jesus asks if he believes and to which he responds, "Lord I believe, help my unbelief" (Mk 9:25). Faith in God is like a muscle in the body, it is through exercise that it grows stronger. Part of being human is recognising that at times our "spiritual means" will not be great; but simply by living with as much faith as we can muster our capacity to trust increases in strength and vigour.

As many of you will know from experience, childhood uncertainties about the trustworthiness of significant others have implications for our life of faith even though we might not be conscious of their influence. However, these memories stored within the personality hover like spectres in the recesses of consciousness and come to torment us in the early hours of the morning. It is with incredulity that in the bright light of the morning we recognise them for what they are - spectres, things devoid of substance. We say to ourselves things like, "I don't know where that came from because it is so very different from what I actually believe".

However, at some level of your being it is what you believe. It is a part of you that has been long forgotten but a part whose childish sentiments and beliefs still exercises an influence upon you.

All of us recognise that a child has to say goodbye to childhood in order to be an adolescent as the adolescent must die to adolescence in order to be an adult. I don't believe that any of us would object to the notion of us changing as people but most, if not all of us, live our lives in a different way. We strive for the kind of security that as an adult is not only impossible to achieve but also inappropriate to our adult needs. Instead of being content with sufficient security we try to engineer a level of security that is impossible to find and thus open ourselves to inevitable disappointment.

In adulthood I believe that all of us have difficulty in accepting the fact of our non-being and the diminutions that occur through illness, old age and death. Insecurity in early childhood, and which one of us has ever had a totally secure upbringing, can make it difficult for us to let go of all that we love in this world, people, places, things. But let go of them we must if we are to respond to the promptings of the Spirit to grow and change as people.

God has ways of bringing the lives of each of us to its full potential (Jn 10:10) and these moments are generally at the more difficult times of our lives. What happens is that in moments of our surrender to "what is", God can correct all the mistakes we have made, all the opportunities we missed during the earlier part of our lives. All that is required is for us to learn to be present to reality for it is only in reality that we can find Reality.

Prayer is a practice that schools us in the art of living whereby we learn to both accept and let go of the gifts given by God. In short, we learn to live by faith that we shall receive what we need but only when we need it. In the crisis moments of our lives we are being asked to take another look at our hesitations and to realise that these hesitations were based upon our inability to handle life's events at a particular moment of our lives, a moment long since past. The challenge is for us to learn to live in the Now for only the now is real, the past is a memory the future a fantasy – only the now is real.

I won't pretend that I am an expert in the art of living in the now but my twenty five years of meditation have at least made me aware of my tendency to live in either the past or the future. Some people who practice the prayer of quiet speak of the calmness their practice brings them in times of crisis. I am pleased for them that this is the case but it's not the case with me. The way of silence is for me a way of aligning all that I am upon that of God in me and is therefore a process that involves pain and struggle.

Prayer gives me the courage to say, "Amen" – "would that it might be so" to difficult situations that I need to face or accept. I would also like to say that such a prayer is made with good grace but this too would be a lie. However, it is always made with as much faith and courage as I can muster but always conscious of how lacking I am in either of these qualities.

It would be easy at this point to give myself a hard time for being such a limited and flawed human being. However, to do so would be to fly in the face of Christian wisdom and tradition. "My grace is sufficient for you, power is made perfect in weakness" (2 Cor. 12:9) St Paul reports as being the response of Christ to his request for healing of his "thorn in the flesh". Like Paul I am content with my weakness for it is in the "stable" of my weakness that the Christ is to be born not in the "palace" of falsity that part of me would like to build as a more "suitable" dwelling for the Divine.

In my last letter I mentioned that I would be giving a talk here in Tayport on the 26th of August. As you will appreciate given my present state of health, combined with measures that may be necessary to stabilise it, this may not be possible. However, let us proceed on the basis that the talk will take place until I know for sure that it won't be possible to honour the commitment.

Please keep me in your heart as I keep you all in mine.

My Dear Friends,

Since my last letter to you life has not been altogether easy due to a slight deterioration in my health. I have had infections, and viruses but I am glad to be able to say that these have now gone and I am feeling much better. My breathing is easy and I feel that I have once again "bounced" back to what for me is a good state of health.

I went to the hospital today to meet with my consultant only to find that owing to an accident my usual consultant is unable to take her clinics for a least a week. Another consultant was taking her place today and it was he who informed me that a recent scan indicated that my cancer has now spread to the surface of my heart. Happily other tests revealed that my heart is functioning well and there is very little fluid building up as a result of the cancers spread. The stand-in consultant suggested that the condition of my heart be monitored by further tests within the next month and offered an appointment with my regular consultant in five weeks time.

However, it is possible that my own consultant on her return to work in the next week or two may suggest further chemotherapy. This makes it difficult for me to know if a course of treatment may or may not be suggested to me and therefore still difficult for me to make plans for the future. Because of this uncertainty I feel it necessary to cancel the talk I promised to give at Tayport on the 26th of August. I know that this will disappoint many of you who were hoping to be there but late cancellation of this Tayport event would be very difficult; owing to a number of you travelling a long distance to the event. I would hope that all might understand the reasons for this cancellation and, as you will appreciate, I regret that this course of action should have proved necessary.

As well as this being a slightly difficult period health-wise it has also been an emotionally difficult period. I say this because I have become increasingly aware of distressing details appertaining to asbestos related illnesses and claims for compensation. Whilst I do not believe it to be true that there are some things in life it is better not to know, I do believe that some knowledge can make life more uncomfortable.

To cut a very long story short, I have been in correspondence with the firm of solicitors who are representing me in my claim for damages against my former employers. In a recent communication with them I raised the question as to why my former trade union was not also liable due to the effects of asbestos being in the public forum for some time before its banning. After some prompting I received a letter stating that whilst the point I raise is an interesting one they do not consider that the Unions have a case to answer. They further state that since they represent my former Union they would be unable to act on my behalf should I ever have evidence sufficient to take them to court. Whilst understanding their inability to act on my behalf in such proceedings I am far from convinced that the trade unions in the factory can be said to have no degree of culpability in this matter. As I see it they had a duty of protection to their members and failed in that duty by not responding to information that was in the public forum for a number of years.

Owing to the growing number of asbestos deaths, in 1928 the British Government had commissioned Edward Merewether, a Medical Inspector of Factories, and Charles Price, an Engineering Inspector, to prepare a study of the health of those working in the asbestos textile industry. The report was published in 1930 and showed that around one-quarter of their sample of workers (95) had asbestosis and 21 more had early signs of the disease. After a period of twenty years, four out of five workers still in the industry had asbestosis. Their findings gave rise to The Asbestos Industry regulations (1931) which were introduced to control the now known to be hazardous asbestos dust.

Though the link between asbestos and cancer had not been established at that time there is more than sufficient evidence to show how dangerous a substance asbestos is. What is more these findings were in the public forum and would or should have been known to the Unions. As I see it they were either negligent in spotting the danger of this substance to their members or were reluctant to act due to the massive redundancies that would have taken place should this material have been banned. Asbestos was such an important substance in most of British industry that it would have been very tempting for all parties to have traded a few lives for the general wellbeing of the populace.

The mesothelioma explosion only began in the 1960's but the ill effects of asbestos dust were known at the turn of the century. As early as 1906, a government committee had requested information on the prevalence of asbestosis amongst workers after the death of an unknown patient of Dr Montague Murray, a physician at the Charring Cross Hospital London, in 1900 : but the TUC were unable to provide it. Over the last century there were a variety of reasons as to why trade unions failed to respond to the health and safety needs of their members. But perhaps the principle reason was that they were inclined to place jobs above health. It is also interesting to note that those rank and file trade unionists that fought a lone campaign for better safety measures and compensation in the 1960's were side lined by their unions. However, the culpability of the Unions was not as great as that of the employers who misled, bullied and browbeat all who seemed to prevent them furthering their own purposes and designs.

Since developing mesothelioma I have been profoundly shocked by the way in which we mesothelioma sufferers have been and still are being used by others. For example, I will possibly get as compensation from Turner Newall, my former employers who are in receivership, something in the region of between 15 – 60p in the pound compensation. However, the company sent in as administrator for T&N is making millions in fees. Kroll Buchler Phillips, the administrators of the compensation fund, has charged £17 million in fees to date and their solicitors have charged £6 million. All of these vast sums of money have been removed from funds available for the compensation of us mesothelioma victims.

Similarly law firms do quite well in their pursuance of claims on behalf of those of us fated to die from this terrible industrial disease. A number of firms of solicitors make sufficient profit from fees made in the pursuance of mesothelioma claims as to be able to support the work of the asbestos charities that in turn provide them with a client base. From my viewpoint, which I grant you is limited, it would seem as if everyone is doing well out of this industrial disease apart from those of us whose lives has been cut short by illness.

I am sorry to say that this sordid business gets even worse as the Canadian Government is still promoting the use and sale of white asbestos.

More than 90% of global asbestos consumption is chrysotile (white asbestos); Canada is one of the world's largest chrysotile producers exporting more than 95% of the annual fibre output. The use of asbestos, including chrysotile, is banned or seriously restricted in most industrial countries because its safe use is considered to be unrealistic.

At the same time as asbestos is being removed from government buildings on Capital Hill, Ottawa, proposals to promote the use of chrysotile in Canadian public buildings and infrastructures are being considered. Abroad Canadian asbestos stakeholders are aggressively promoting the use of chrysotile in developing countries where appropriate controls and regulation do not exist. Canada promotes the sale of chrysotile through the Montreal-based Asbestos Institute (AI); between 1984-2001, the A.I. received a total of $54 million, two thirds of which came from public funds.

However, I am happy to report that a Canadian Member of Parliament, Pat Martin from Manitoba, spoke out against Canada's support for the industry he calls a "corporate serial killer." He went on to say, ""While the rest of the developed world is banning asbestos in all its forms, Canada is busy exporting over 220,000 tonnes per year into under-developed and Third World countries where health and safety regulations are non-existent or not enforced, thereby exposing millions of ill-informed and unsuspecting people to its hazards."

But why should I concern myself with these things at a time when reason might suggest that the time might be better employed in more "spiritual" pursuits? Why should I write letters to politicians that largely seem to go un-noticed or misunderstood? Why should I spend time and effort trying to get others interested in the injustice meted out to those suffering from mesothelioma? The answer is because I see power being used against people rather than for them.

However, there is a use of power which is particularly divine and lovely: the power to protect and support the powerless. To use the power of your body to help the weak; to use the power of your mind to help the less gifted; to use the power of your heart to comfort, strengthen, and support those in pain and distress is to live a holy life. A spirituality that is not rooted in compassion, a "suffering with" the other is highly suspect. It is because Christ carried the cross for each of us that we must bear our own cross and one another's crosses. We must learn to use our power for others rather than against others, just as Jesus did.

What I see is not pleasant gripped as it is in the influence of individual moral failings and what St Paul describes as the Principalities and Powers (Col 1:16-17) of this world. A company, a union, a government and even a Church is in constant need of being reminded that it exists to serve values beyond itself. Even that great advocate of the capitalist system Adam Smith acknowledged this when he wrote that the ultimate goal of a business is not to make a profit. Profit is just the means. The goal is the general welfare: institutions do not exist for themselves.

There is a false consciousness, which is part of the human condition, which places me and my "needs" at the centre of the world rather than God. This false consciousness infects every aspect of our being, even our spirituality. Today, as in the time of Amos, the Old Testament prophet of social justice, many are concerned only with their spiritual "enlightenment" and their own private world. Many present day philosophies fail to take us beyond the narcissism of our natural self-centredness, being solely concerned with our "enlightenment".

Authentic prayer is inseparable from prophesy. Time without number those of you who have attended my talks will have heard me say that the practice of contemplative prayer enables one to see what is there, not what we think is there want to be there but actually is there. Sometimes one is unsettled by what one sees, distressed or frightened by what one sees but this is the price to be paid for deep prayer.

As we know, the path to the experience of unity and love is a path of self surrender, a dying so as to live. But the dying of the ego is more than withdrawal of ego activity as experienced in activities such as meditation or contemplation. It is an event that shakes us to our roots. It's a stepping out of the structures and patterns that are comfortable and we have grown fond of; structures and patterns that give us a sense of security.

Prayer ultimately leads to unity and peace but that is a final goal not an immediate one. The temptation is to indulge into what the third century monks of the desert called the "pernicious peace", a peace achieved through repression and wilful blindness; a refusal to embrace the reality of one's own life and one's world. The human condition is one of incompleteness and therefore cannot but involve struggle. It requires the facing of hard facts about oneself and one's world and a shouldering of a burden that at times feels heavy.

In order to be a spiritual person it is first of all essential to become humanized; in touch with the totality of your own being and in touch with reality, the reality that you see and the reality that you don't see. We become saints not through our spiritual practices, though these are important, but by letting life "do it" to us. If you try to manage it you can guarantee that you will end up in a mess – you can't sanctify yourself. If you let life change you, by simply responding to what comes to you joy or sorrow, you can have a "goddened" existence. God's love can only come into the world if there are people who are prepared to incarnate that love, give it form and "Be Christ Today".

Many thanks to those of you whose 'phone calls, prayers and good wishes do so much to sustain me on this stage of my life's journey. May God reward you for your kindness and generosity.

My Dear Friends,

Saturday the 23rd of September saw me wakening early in the morning with a generalised feeling of sadness. Of late this has happened several times and has led to teary episodes where "loss" has been the central theme.

Loss of fitness and strength are the obvious losses but there is also the loss that afflicts anyone with a serious illness and that is the loss of "place". If one is by reason of illness or death removed from ones "place" within the family, occupation or social situation the gap left by ones absence quickly heals over. After a while it is as if one had never even been there. Such awareness brings with it the recognition of ones insignificance in the world's order; a realisation the world can manage quite well without one. I have spoken often on the subject of egocentricity and its tendency to dominate our lives, it came as a shock therefore to realise how much of a grip it still has on me. I realise that I am not on my own in this respect for all of us can be deluded about their feelings of indispensability and worth to the world. I like the rest of humankind am in a state of incompletion but journeying towards fulfilment in the Lord.

At a recent meeting with my oncologist I was sharing with her some of these moments when "loss" has been very much to the fore along with the sadness that such feelings engender. She knowingly smiled and said that such thoughts were common in one who was in my situation and said that they were known as "anticipatory grief" – part of the emotional roller-coaster that is terminal cancer.

Over the last couple of months my breathing has become more laboured when exercising and a recent echocardiogram indicated fluid had once again started to build up around my heart. When this happens it constricts my heart, makes it more difficult for it to expand, and consequently makes for breathing difficulties. When I saw the oncologist she was concerned by the level of fluid revealed on an x-ray taken on the day of my appointment and so she contacted the cardiology department for further investigation of this condition.

The cardiologist ordered another echocardiogram to ascertain more accurately the level of fluid but decided, after viewing the results, that it would be better to wait till the fluid level had increased before draining it off. In the meantime the cardiologist considered a monitoring of the situation the most appropriate course of action. As I understand it, there is a limit to the number of times that it is possible to drain fluid from the heart and so it becomes imperative to wait till the level increases. The removal of fluid would increase the quality of my life immediately but this has to be weighed against the risks involved in the procedure and the number of occasions the task can be performed. However, should there be a sudden deterioration in my breathing I can always go back to the hospital knowing that any difficulties I have will always be taken seriously.

When I left the hospital my major feeling was one of relief at not being referred to a heart surgeon, a possibility previously discussed, for the creation of a pericardial window in my heart to drain out the fluid. I was also more than glad not to have been kept in hospital for the procedure necessary to remove the fluid around my heart. Whilst I know that this would bring almost immediate relief from breathlessness it is an unpleasant procedure that is, in my opinion, best avoided if at all possible! Hence the feeling of relief!

It was only a couple of days later when I woke up feeling a wee bit sad that I realised that in my meeting with the oncologist there was no mention of the chemotherapy that had been discussed with me at an earlier date, neither was there a mention of the possibility of heart surgery. Whilst neither of these two things were attractive to me, especially the heart surgery, it was only on reflection that I realised that previous treatment possibilities no longer seemed to have had a place in our discussions.

Sometimes what is not said to one is more significant than what is said and on this occasion I believe this to be the case. In our conversation there was no mention of stabilising my condition only a discussion on how I might die: a subject that was raised by me. Despite this conversation and no plan of intervention I left the hospital feeling euphoric. However, something in me knew the truth of my situation without the circumstances of it ever percolating through to my conscious mind and that is why I believe I woke up on the 23rd with a feeling of sadness. This feeling of sadness has to do with the fact that I now believe that my situation has changed to one of palliative care; I have left the plateau of stable health that has been mine for so long.

I remember writing in a previous letter, Letter16, about my physical condition as it was then and likening the situation to the anxiety I used to have prior to my running in a race:-

A few years ago I used to love to run in long distance road races. Though I say it myself, I was quite an accomplished runner and always in the top twenty per cent of any field. No matter how often I took part in races I always used to find the wait for the starting gun to go off the most difficult part of the race. During that time all the self doubt I had over my performance would come flooding into consciousness; had I prepared well enough; had I over trained and become too tired; were the laces on my shoes too tight or too slack; was the slight discomfort I felt in my shin going to prevent me from completing the course, etc.

Though I was with thousands of other runners I always had a great sense of aloneness realising that everything was down to me, no one could run the race for me. These were anxious moments and moments that I always dreaded; dreaded more than the pain and difficulty of competing in a long race. However, after the starting pistol had been fired all the anxiety faded away, the nervous energy went into my legs and away I went! I was then able to let go of my fantasies about the race, my fitness and problems I might have during the race. All I had to do was get round the course as fast as I could. On each and every occasion I took part in a race I discovered that this anticipatory period of fantasy prior to the race was always more of a problem than the actual race. This discovery taught me a valuable lesson in life that when we face a demanding or possibly painful situation the anticipation of it tends to be more difficult than the actual situation itself.

At the moment in this the "limbo" of my present life I can see a similitude between pre-race anxiety and my present state of health. When I hear that my cancer has once again started to grow a small part of me will, despite my love of life, be glad that it is now time to face what I fear. The power of human imagination is such that reality is seldom as awful as the imagined scenario. I do not fear death but I do fear the process of dying with its loss of independence and discomfort but I also know, through my running, that it is my fear and self doubt that have the greatest capacity to disable me. Reality, no matter how difficult, is always our friend and the more we are grounded in our own reality the safer we are; it is all too easy for us human beings to get lost in the "what ifs".

I now feel that the "starting pistol" has been fired and whilst the anticipatory anxiety has gone it has been replaced with an anxiety about being able to stay the course. Embracing a new reality is never easy especially when that reality is the harbinger of ones own death. But face it I must and face it with as much courage as I can for it is only in embracing the things that frighten us that they can give us their blessing.

Some time ago I read, "Cancer is God's gift to the one who has everything". At first glance this seemed to be a sick joke and quite the most ridiculous thing I had ever read. However, on reflection I began to see what the person might be trying to say by making such a shocking statement. Perhaps what the person was trying to say in such an outrageous statement is that a person like me who has been very fortunate in those they have loved and been loved by find it hard to leave behind all they hold dear.

The Christian teaching on detachment helps towards making a good death but how difficult it is for one as richly blessed as I to let go of all the good friends I have made over the years. Christianity, through the teachings of Jesus, shows us how to be good "losers" – how to hold all things and all people lightly and not cling. How to relish whatever is given one in terms of worldly goods and friendships without clinging to them.

For many years I have spoken about acquiring the skill of caring and not caring; of the need to hold people and things lightly; of the need to live in the "now" and not be over concerned about the future. I have given many talks and retreats on these and allied themes but now have to journey towards the "practicum": move ever closer to the reality rather than the notion of these concepts. I am more convinced than ever that we become saints not through our spiritual practices, though these are important, but by letting life "do it" to us. I pray that I may have the courage and faith to live my life to its fullness and continue to grow in God until my last breath.

I would once again ask you to keep me in your heart and mind as I enter this new and exciting stage of my life. On the fourth of October I will be going to the hospital to speak to medical students on the subject of death and dying so if you can remember to say a "wee" prayer for me on that day I would be very grateful. As you will appreciate, doing this will not be too easy but I hope that it will be beneficial to both them and to me.

I have written a couple of very brief essays on Mary the Mother of God. If you would like to have a copy of these please make your request known to me. I hope to spend a few days with my sister this coming week so do not be too surprised if I do not respond to your request immediately.

Many thanks for your kind messages of support and encouragement. Right from the start of this illness I have always maintained that I can cope with anything if I have the love and support of good friends and the compassionate skill of medical personnel. Up to now I feel supported in both aspects of my requirements and this gives me the faith to trust more deeply the Eleventh Hour God. He is a God who provides what is needed when it is needed and never a moment before that time!

My Dear Friends,

I know that it has been only a few weeks since my last letter but once again the inner compulsion to write is upon me and so here is letter twenty one!

As I have explained on several occasions, I write these letters whenever something strikes me as being important or significant. But not only that, I write as a means of understanding what I know and sharing with you what I hope are insights into life and living. In this particular letter the latter point about needing to put on paper personal understanding that has come to me is very important

The last week or so has been a challenging time for me but one in which I feel I have acquitted myself well. The first of the challenges that faced me was that of speaking to a group of medical students in the oncology department of Ninewells Hospital about death and dying. I felt privileged in being asked to do this and though I knew it would not be easy I was keen to embrace the task.

There were about fifteen to twenty students present and all of them listened attentively and kept me furnished with good and sensible questions for an hour and a half. As you will appreciate, the answers to these questions were not hypothetical but based upon my own personal experience of life and coming to terms with my own diminution. The session left me feeling exhausted but fulfilled; especially after hearing from my oncologist that she felt the lives of the young people would have been changed forever by the session.

A few days later I decided to undertake a task that had been hovering about in the back of my mind for several weeks – arranging my funeral. Yes, I know that this may sound slightly maudlin to some of you but the motivating factor was a duty of care for those I will leave behind. It was an exercise that, along with every other friar in our Province, I completed several years ago but I felt the need to re-appraise what I had written.

There were practical things to attend to as well as my own funeral liturgy to organise – hymns, readings, readers, prayers, etc. All of this I was able to do with a degree of detachment but when it came to writing instructions about what was to take place at the graveside the tears began to flow. The exercise had moved from being an organisational task to being that of an impending event. This was, of course, a right and healthy thing to happen but such deliberations also had something of the "surreal" about them.

During the last few weeks I heard of a degree of callousness and lack of sensitivity shown by members of staff at two hospices; one of one of them in which I will probably spend my last days. As you can imagine this was not a pleasant thing to hear but it is part of a reality that needs to be faced. However, it should be mentioned that the persons from whom these stories sprang had nothing but praise for the ethos of the hospices and the kindness shown the vast majority of the staff in these institutions. The complaints were against specific individuals and once the complaint had been made to the authorities it was treated with the seriousness warranted by such situations.

I know that from time to time all institutions fall short of their aims and aspirations and know too that it is only by relatives and friends complaining that the reinstatement of appropriate standards can take place. I know my relatives and friends well enough to know that even when I am unable to defend myself they will always look to my comfort and wellbeing. It therefore follows that I need have no fear of any kind of insensitivity or abuse in hospital or hospice. However, despite my knowing and believing this I was taken by surprise over the amount of anger I had towards those members of staff that had fallen short of the mark in the hospices.

I also knew that my reactions were what one might call, "over the top" but still they persisted; despite my knowing that when my time came to let go of life I would not be short of "defenders" should they ever be needed. Furthermore I also knew from my therapeutic experience that when one overreacts, as I was now doing, it is a sure sign that something has touched one deeply and profoundly in the inner recesses of the mind.

Even those of us with the most limited psychological insight would know that none of us have had a perfect start in life. As a result of genes and parenting deficits all of us carry within us a degree of vulnerability which for the greater part of our lives we manage to conceal from ourselves and others. The kind of vulnerability we have may vary from person to person in type and manner of expression but it is ours and we have to find a way of coping with it. Again the manner in which we cope with our personality deficits will vary from person to person. Ideally, painful life experiences teach us a way of coping whereby we don't keep repeating patterns of behaviour that damage ourselves and others. If we don't learn to do this then we are fated to repeat destructive patterns of behaviour till we learn life's message!

As I look back upon the life of my parents I see two good but very vulnerable people who, for a number of reasons, failed to develop a sense of inner security within themselves. It was little wonder therefore that they were unable to pass on to me a sense that the world, despite the way it might feel from time to time, is essentially a secure place. As a consequence I learned, like many others in a similar situation, to work hard at creating my own security. Part of this was learning the art of being a "good parent" to myself, being tolerant of my failures and personality defects, learning to calm my own fears and encouraging myself to face new challenges and situations. This strategy has helped me to live a worthwhile life and a life that I like to think has brought benefits to many others also.

However, I now feel that this stratagem, an approach that has proven dividends in the past, is failing and it is time for it to be abandoned. As my health slowly begins to decline I will become weaker and frailer. I will once again return to the state of dependency that was mine as a child – a state in which I did not experience security. The thoughts of returning to a state of being that one found frightening is a sure trigger for strong feelings of anger; anger whose purpose is that of establishing order and making the world safe.

When any feeling, such as being dependent, is felt to be dangerous, fear may repress the emotion into the unconscious, where it continues to express itself surreptitiously in illness or in less than healthy forms of behaviour. Analysis or other forms of psychological treatment may make one aware of the existence of such a complex and devise strategies of enabling one to deal with it but still it remains within one: all that happens is that one gets better at coping with it.

It is as if one had within one a basic fault, a fault not like a moral fault but a geological fault, which suddenly becomes active when something aggravates the tectonic plates of the psyche. In my case it was the thoughts of being helpless and dependant upon others who might not behave appropriately that activated feelings of insecurity and set the tectonic plates moving. Such thoughts brought to mind the lack of security experienced in an early stage of my life when the world felt unsafe. The anger I experienced was a reaction against the feelings of helplessness and the desire to make life safe for myself, a strategy I have employed for many years. However, I now realise that to be an authentic and whole person I have no choice other than to learn to trust more profoundly than I have ever done in the past to the goodness that is in human nature. This is no time for strategies but a time for faith and the possibility of a remedial experience as a healing balm for my vulnerability and lack of trust.

In my last letter I wrote, "I am more convinced than ever that we become saints not through our spiritual practices, though these are important, but by letting life "do it" to us." If ever there was need of evidence to the truth of the above statement the dawning realisation of the opportunities that lie before me are proof positive. What has happened is that Life has steered me once again in a direction I would rather not go. But the exciting thing is that all I have to do is let Life "do it" to me, in order to be transformed, healed, restored.

Those of you who have heard the many talks I have given on prayer will know that on our spiritual journey we are invited to dismantle the false self and the strategies we have employed for repressing parts of us that in the past we found difficult to cope with. You will know too how often I have spoken of the Holy Spirit's tendency to keep wakening up bits of us that we would rather keep asleep! As our trust in God grows the strategies we have employed to cope with life no longer are seen to be an essential means of survival. Each major life event provides us with an opportunity to learn to further trust Life rather than our coping mechanisms.

The practice of pure prayer, a simple attentiveness, is a great aid in this task but Life offers a remedial experience that is both frightening and challenging. God allows this process because he is determined to bring healing and wholeness to our damaged fragmented selves. He is not content to let us be less than we are capable of being. All that is required of us is to ascend to a process, a process of becoming, and learn to be content with a limited degree of security, independence and trust of others. The overcoming of emotional distortion is part of Gods plan for us because he is never happy with us being half alive.

I find it exciting that even though it would appear that my body is declining in strength God works so deeply and profoundly to heal aspects of my personality. How ironic it is that at this late stage of my life God has not given up on me but instead challenges me to become greater than I ever imagined possible. The time that is left to me is a special time, a time of fecundity and newness despite all the difficulties associated with health and mobility. I pray that I might not waste this experience but always respond with as much faith and courage as I can muster.

I have an echocardiogram on the 18th of the month and the results of this will determine if the fluid around my heart needs to be drained off. As I have said in the past this is a far from pleasant experience and not without its risks but it is a treatment that brings swift relief to the kind of breathing difficulties I have.

I have also been asked if I would be willing to give a further interview for medical students on the subject of death and dying on the 24th of October. The plan is to video this interview and use it as a teaching aid for medical students and junior doctors. As I said above, I find giving an interview on this subject a difficult experience but one that is infinitely worthwhile if it can bring about greater understanding of those who have a terminal condition. For this reason I have accepted to give this interview.

Once again I would ask you to keep me in your heart, as I keep you in mine, not just on those two dates but throughout the time left to me. Every good wish to you all.

My Dear Friends,

Once again the date of my birthday has come around. It used to be that birthdays were part of the ordinary round of life, apart from the gifts and cards arising from the generosity of friends. It is true that the decades of one's life might be occasions that afforded a greater celebration than customary but on the whole birthdays used to come and go with little more than the simple greeting, "Many Happy Returns of the day".

Well, that used to be the case with me but since the diagnosis of terminal cancer and, at that time, a life expectancy of no more than twelve months, each birthday I celebrate feels as if I am cheating Death. For the last three birthday celebrations there has always been a reminder of my own mortality and the recognition that there will not be "Many Happy Returns of the day".

Last year, on my sixtieth birthday, I was in the departure lounge of Belfast Airport when I decided to check my e-mails only to find that a friend had, for accuracies sake, sent to me a draft of an obituary that is to appear on the Christian Meditation website on my demise. In relating this event in one of my Letters I wrote:-

As you can possibly imagine, this generated in me a maelstrom of emotions with feelings oscillating between happiness and sadness. It was not the obituary that caused the upset because the feelings were already there: the obituary was simply the trigger to ill defined emotions that had been mine for several days beforehand.

Well, it seems to be the case that the "maelstrom of emotions" that have been mine around the time of my recent birthdays is, true to form, still weaving its spell. Just before my birthday this year I went to visit two young friends who had recently received the gift of two delightful twin girls, Sian and Thea. It was wonderful to see the two girls, who were no more than a week old, but more delightful still to see the selfless love their parents had for them. I have given many, many talks on selflessness but seeing the love and courageous commitment of the parents to these two helpless bundles of love far outweighed any talk or homily I could give. It was the love of the parents that started the journey of the twins into life and it will be the same love that will bring their lives into maturity and fruition.

On the day I saw the children my emotions were close to the surface. I was deeply and profoundly struck by the fact that here were two little people beginning the journey of their life and here was I drawing to the close of mine. To hold new life in your arms whilst painfully aware of how one's own life is slowly and resolutely draining into the sands of time is difficult and yet at the same time there is "rightness" about it.

The two girls are very different in looks and personality and whilst I was holding the more fractious of the two, Sian, in my arms she fell into a secure and contented repose. In my therapeutic work with others I have held the fractious child in so many who suffered and sought my help as a balm for their condition. I held in them a part of their personality which was frightened and alone, a part of them that was troubled and sad. This I did in the hope that they would learn from me how to accept, hold and value in their personalities what initially they felt to be an affliction, a trouble. In that moment of holding this particular child, Sian, I felt between the two of us here was a living symbol of what my life for the past thirty years had been about. It was an absolute joy to me that this child found comfort in my arms and I found in that moment a validation of all that I had tried to do and aspired to be in my life; the fulfilment of a lifelong work well done.

Another powerful emotion that was mine was that of gratitude. I was full of thankfulness for having seen the child's parents marry, something I did not feel I would live long enough to see. But not only had I been granted such a privilege, here I was holding the fruit of their love in my arms. I was aware too that it is time to pass on the baton of incarnating God's love to others and in this I was reminded of the words of Simeon in Luke's Gospel who, whilst holding the Christ child in his arms says, "At last, all powerful Master you give leave to your servant to go in peace, according to your promise." (Lk2:29)

Simeon said these words without regret; knowing, as he did, that the time had come for him to let go of life. This he learned to do in the surety of knowing that he had completed his vocation as a prophet and a true follower of God. It was time for him to pass on to others the baton of faith and belief in the one true God. Nothing had gone wrong; everything was as it should be, and it was simply time for a new incarnation of God's love in the world. Throughout the course of my life I have aspired to be an incarnation of that love in our world: the work will continue after I am gone, the means of bringing about the "becoming" of God simply changes.

However, whilst believing all of the above I also believe that there are still duties of care that are still mine. There is growth, both spiritual and psychological, to accomplish and teaching to be communicated which, if required, might need the use of words. Without doubt the last two and a half years of my life, whilst being the most difficult, have also been the happiest and most fecund I have ever experienced. One of the great blessings I have had in speaking to medical students about the process of living with a terminal illness has been the opportunity to reflect upon the process of living and dying. The gently probing questions of my oncologist and her students provided the catalyst to not only the process of reflection but also to the awaking of affectivity one would expect to accompany such reflection.

At the moment all my feelings seem to be very accessible and close to the surface and so, from time to time I find myself almost overpowered by feelings of gratitude, love and sorrow. One of the questions asked of me during the above interview was whether I had ever felt depressed since being diagnosed with mesothelioma. In reply to that question I said that depression had to do with not feeling the intensity of one's affect whilst what I was experiencing had to do with feeling things, both joy and sorrow, too much. What is happening within me is a simple "coming home" to who and how I am. It is a process that involves loss and therefore sorrow but with the loss comes a joyful clarity of perception as to what is and is not important in life. This is the quiet joy of loving and knowing oneself to be loved; therein is true riches to be found.

There is an old joke that says that an Englishman takes pride in being a self made man – a task that relieves God of a fearsome responsibility! However, whilst the joke is made at the expense of we English it is important that all of us recognise the tendency lurking within us to be the creators of ourselves. It is a tendency that is not restricted to a particular race or class but part of the human condition. The uncomfortable truth is that there are certain things that are out of our control and in these circumstances or situations we can only respond with faith or trust. Whilst Jesus tells us that his yoke is easy and his burden light (Mt. 11:30) we also need to remember that he tells us to pick up his cross and follow him (Mt. 16:24).

The cross is not always easy to shoulder and at times the burden will not feel light, and there will be times when we will be unsure if we can bear its weight. However, if we rail against the carrying of whatever cross comes our way we, in our protest, actually increase the burden that we have to carry. This is so because we then carry not just the thing that afflicts us but the resentment over seeing ourselves as victim. But no matter what our affliction carry it we must and learn to do so with as much good grace as we can manage.

However, this is always painful and requires that we let go of our best loved pictures of ourselves, our achievements and our abilities. These are the things that we have wrapped around ourselves to give us a sense of "solidity", security and esteem. Living without these constructs can make life feel hellish but the real hell comes from trying to defend oneself from the labour of preserving a false self from the reality and the experience of everyday living.

We need to step back from the collective fantasy in which I try to decide who I am, try to persuade you to affirm the image I have of myself and even try to use God as a reinforcement for my picture of myself. All of us need to be coaxed by God into the honesty of being who we are rather than the accomplished and self contained person we pretend to be.

A person like me who has been very fortunate in those they have loved and been loved by finds it hard to leave behind all they hold dear. However, the grieving in leaving behind the things, places and people one loves is proof positive that one has fulfilled the Divine command to love and as such it is a sweet and noble pain to endure. It is this realisation that makes the yoke of Christ easy and his burden light (Mt. 11:30).

On a more factual and practical level, I am awaiting tests to see if I have sufficient fitness to undergo heart surgery to relieve the pressure of fluid around my heart. At a recent case conference it was suggested that I have a small "window" cut into the outer layer of my heart tissue which would facilitate the draining of fluid not only now but in the future too. The removal of fluid by a catheter into the heart, which was the way the fluid was previously drained off, is a somewhat dangerous procedure, given the location of the fluid. It is therefore thought best to undertake this surgical procedure which can probably be done with keyhole surgery so as to give a better quality of life. As you can imagine, I do not look forward to the possibility of this procedure, which will have to be done in Edinburgh, but consider it to be another part of the process of "abandonment" to which I need to learn to submit.

Please keep me close to your heart as I keep you close to mine. There is no substitute for the love and support of trusted friends when one is oneself a little more vulnerable than one has been accustomed to in the past. Many thanks to those of you who tell me that these letters are of some help to you and yours. It is a great comfort to know that even at this stage in my life I can still be of help and service to others.

My Dear Friends,

Yes it is once again time for another letter despite the fact that it was only a two or three weeks since the last missive! What has prompted this letter has been the need for a brief stay in hospital to attend to some troublesome symptoms that I was experiencing.

On Thursday of last week the Macmillan nurse who comes to visit me each week was a little concerned over the deterioration that had taken place in my breathing. As well as this I was suffering coughing fits which constituted a further problem to my being able to catch my breath. As you will appreciate fits of coughing not only prevent one breathing properly but also cause irritation in the throat which in turn causes one to cough, thus constructing a vicious circle which is hard to break with its obvious problems for one's breathing. The nurse, Denise, decided to telephone my oncologist who, on taking the call, suggested that I be admitted to the oncology ward immediately. The purpose of the admission was to ascertain through tests and observation if my difficulties were stemming from a cardiac or pulmonary problem.

After being admitted I was subjected to a whole series of tests and examinations which, to cut a very long story short, revealed that there is now a "shadow" on the inside of my left lung. This lung is the lung whose plural surface is covered by the mesothelioma tumour; a tumour that is steadily thickening with the passing of time. The "shadow" could be a chest infection but having recently had a number of infections that have been treated by antibiotics one is left to wonder precisely what is the nature of the shadowy area within the lung. If it were an infection would the antibiotics not have cleared up the problem? However, whatever condition it is that is manifesting itself it is the difficulties within this lung that were causing the coughing fits. A course of palliative care for the treatment of symptoms and the containment of the new disease process has been worked out and I am feeling much better.

One of the things that was discovered whilst I was in hospital was that the fluid level around my heart still remains the same and its level is such that there would be little quality of life to be gained as a result of attempting to drain it off. Verification of the cardiologist's opinion later came from the surgeon in Edinburgh who had previously agreed, subject to viewing my echocardiograms, to construct a pericardial window in my heart. Just before I left hospital he contacted my oncologist and said that in his opinion, given the present level of fluid around my heart he did not feel that much increase in the quality of my life could be achieved as a result of the proposed surgery.

Part of me was relieved to hear this for though I was more than willing to undergo the surgery to have a better quality of life I had a fear of something going "wrong" after the surgery and being kept in the Edinburgh hospital. I don't like being in any hospital but the idea of being away from the whole panoply of people here in the Dundee/ Fife area that I have grown to trust did produce a degree of fear. Last week when I was unwell, it was a well run network of people and resources came to my aid. For my part I had the trust and security to believe that whatever came my way these people would always do their best for me.

It was this feeling that was with me when I awoke in my own bed on Saturday morning. As I sat up in bed drinking the first cup of tea of the day I realised how fortunate I was and once again was surprised by tears of simple joy and gratitude. I know it might sound a little strange to some of you to read that there is within me a great capacity for joy despite the reality of my demise drawing ever close but this is the case.

The thought of dying is not a frightening thought but from time to time I do become fearful of the process of dying. The experience of last week gave me a quiet joy in the realisation that I will never be alone but always in the company of trusted others who will do their level best to ensure that my passing will be as easy as it can be. Perhaps this is the very best we can hope for at the end time.

Whilst shedding a tear over this wonderful realisation I also began to realise that for me death was not so much an ending but the fulfilment of my life. This I had a glimpse of and wrote about in my last letter when I narrated what happened to me when holding in my arms the child of some young friends. In my last letter I wrote, "I was aware too that it is time to pass on the baton of incarnating God's love to others and in this I was reminded of the words of Simeon in Luke's Gospel who, whilst holding the Christ child in his arms says, "At last, all powerful Master you give leave to your servant to go in peace, according to your promise." (Lk2:29)

Simeon said these words without regret; knowing, as he did, that the time had come for him to let go of life. This he learned to do in the surety of knowing that he had completed his vocation as a prophet and a true follower of God. It was time for him to pass on to others the baton of faith and belief in the one true God. Nothing had gone wrong; everything was as it should be, and it was simply time for a new incarnation of God's love in the world".

Sitting weeping with joy and gratitude the words of Jesus, "Well done, good and faithful servant (Mt 25:23) came into my mind thus confirming a sense of accomplishment, of time well spent. I know that there is still much to be accomplished in the process of learning to conform my life to that of the Divine in me but know too that this change is brought about by a personal loving surrender to God in every detail of my life and living. I have the sense of growing into what I have always been. The journey into Christ has literally become "second nature" to me because it has revealed to me that I have a second nature. This is so because I am becoming less of an individual and more of a person, one who is in union with God, the world and others; bound to all by the bond we call Love.

To many the spiritual life is a life that is hard and ascetic but such sentiments have little resonance in my life. I have tried that course of action and, along with many others, discovered that it has failed me miserably. With maturity has come the realisation that in the spiritual life all we can do is prepare ourselves for the "gift" of new life and expansion of our personality. I think that a suitable image of the kind of spirituality I now write of is my that of a kitten! If you watch a queen cat moving her kittens you will notice that as soon as she picks them up by the scruff of their necks the kittens always go limp. They never struggle against her but let themselves be carried by her confident that she knows what is best for them and knows the place where they will be safe.

Such an approach to the life of the Spirit rids us of the heavy burden of self-justification, self-creation, self-perfection and the need to be a "spiritual" person. This is a theme that can be found in the writings of people so diverse as Martin Luther, St. Therese of Lisieux and the Buddhist teacher Shinran.

Being found in such a variety of people from so many different traditions is, in my opinion, a very strong commendation of it. Enlightenment is something that people strive to attain little realising that it is arriving at the place you are and knowing that there is no need to search for anything for all has been given! All of us need to come to the realisation that God has always been walking in the garden with us and has never been separated from us by anything other than our desire to have life on our own terms.

Another of the gifts I received this weekend was the company of my cousin Alf. who very kindly travelled up from God's country, Lancashire, to see me. He is a fairly frequent visitor and is usually accompanied by his wife and other members of his delightful family. It is always good to see him with others but I think that both of us knew that we needed, on this occasion, to simply spend time together and this we did. I think it would be true to say that as youngsters we were fairly close but for a while the only times we seemed to meet were weddings and funerals.

One of the graces that God has given to me through my illness was the rediscovery of how much Alf and I have in common. Looking at our present closeness one might be tempted to say that there had been a loss of opportunity for intimacy over the years of separation but on reflection I do not believe this to be true. Perhaps both of us needed to change in the way we have in order to meet at a new and more intimate level; nothing can ever be lost or a waste in the life of God.

Whilst we were always close as children our present way of being together and expressing our love for each other required the maturation of something in both of us that could only be accomplished through separateness and the passage of time. When the "fullness of time" had been realised then our coming together was an occasion that brought life, and continues to bring life, to us both. The truth of the matter is that none of us can ever know what is best for us and so simple prudence dictates that we simply try to remain open to the "sacramental moments" that life offers to us and not worry about the rest.

One of the things we discussed over the weekend was life beyond death. Here I feel particularly blessed through my meditation experience for in meditation one can catch a momentary glimpse of a self that lies beyond the flow of conscious thought. This is a self that is forever still, silent and serene no matter how fraught are the superficial concerns of life. With it comes the realisation that I am not my body, my feelings nor my thoughts for these are elements of a time bound world.

Such an intuition brings about the realisation that we have a second nature, one that is rooted in the Divine, is in touch with all other persons and with creation itself. The outer aspects of our self, the form, change with time but there is an essential "is-ness" in all of us that I believe continues beyond the grave. This "is-ness" is the most sacred part of us and is therefore very precious, like gold. Like gold in its molten structure it can assume whatever form is desired of it and has indeed changed its "form" many times throughout out lives: lives punctuated by experiences of mini-deaths and resurrections.

I do not know what lies at the other side of the grave but I am confident that my "is-ness", that which is the essence of who I am in my depths will continue in some form as it has throughout my present life. At this point it would be very easy to get lost in the world of speculative thought but for me it is enough to recall the words from St. John's First Letter, "Beloved, we are God's children now; what we will be has not yet been revealed. What we do know is this: when he is revealed, we will be like him, for we will see him as he is" (1Jn 3:2).

Our religious systems of thought are like computer programmes. Just as the computer can produce no new knowledge outside of its programmes so it is with theological statements unless expanded by mystical experience. By the very simple practice of seeing "what is" new realms and vistas are opened to us and a new perspective on life and living are revealed. This is so because the entire world is sacramental insofar as it both reveals and conceals the Divine. Thus it is that nothing that happens to us is devoid of meaning or potential for growth and life had we but the eyes to see it and the wisdom to appreciate it.

In writing of theological concepts and themes I recall the words of T.S. Eliot in the poem Burnt Norton,

> "Words strain,
> Crack and sometimes break, under the burden,
> Under the tension, slip, slide, perish,
> Decay with imprecision, will not stay in place,
> Will not stay still."

Some of the expressions I have used in this letter for what is commonly referred to as "eternal life" might seem somewhat strange but I would ask you to see them for what they are feeble attempts to "grasp the ungraspable" experiences of a lifetime. The great truths by which we live our lives can never be seen "straight on" but only apprehended by our peripheral sight and therefore only hinted at in the most tangential of ways. It therefore follows that the words needed must be "quarried" from one's life experience rather than concepts contained in a book. I am sorry to say that much religious language I find dull and overused to such an extent that the meaning behind the words can no longer be said to convey the kind of meaning for which the heart craves. Not for nothing does St Francis of Assisi call upon us to preach the Gospel and if necessary use words!

Life is good but not always easy so please continue to keep me in your hearts as I keep you in mine.

My Dear Friends,

Receiving another letter from me after just a week may come as something of a shock to some of you. The reason for this letter has to do with my having had another unexpected period of hospitalisation.

Happily the time spent in hospital was minimal before the symptoms of my breathlessness and stupendously high pulse rate could be controlled. I am very much aware that at this stage of my illness the emphasis is on symptom control and doing whatever is possible to enhance the quality of life available to me. These sudden and unplanned admissions to hospital are occurring with ever increasing frequency and the message of what they mean in terms of life expectancy is not lost on me.

Without a doubt I am very much aware of my own mortality and increasing physical vulnerability. It is with regret that I realise that the solitary life which has been my aim and aspiration for so long is now becoming more and more difficult if not impossible. However, I am gifted with good family and friends who are prepared not only to support me in my everyday living but also afford me the space and time I need for myself. How long it will be before I make the journey to "the other shore" I do not know but I am very much aware of how quickly and easily my health deteriorates. Totally independent living is now impossible for me but those close to me handle the new and strange situations that we face with unbounded kindness and sensitivity. As always, the most difficult thing for me is accepting the fact that I can and do make so much pain for myself by fighting reality instead of learning to simply accept it!

The art of letting go, learning to be a "good looser" has been a common theme in these letters and over the past few days this theme has had a poignancy such as never before. About a week ago I came across an extract from the writings of George Tyrrell, a former Jesuit priest who lived over a hundred years ago and whose writings finally led to his excommunication from the Roman Catholic Church. The text that so touched me was about the evening prayer of Tenebrae (Matins and Lauds for the last three days of Holy Week), when all the candles are slowly extinguished except for the highest of all.

"As at Tenebrae, one after another the lights are extinguished, till one alone - and the highest of all - is left, so it is often with the soul and her guiding stars. In our early days there are many - parents, teachers, friends, books, authorities - but, as life goes on, one by one they fail and leave us in deepening darkness, with an increasing sense of the mystery and inexplicability of all things, till at last none but the figure of Christ stands out luminous against the prevailing night."

I am so profoundly aware of how further letting go into Christ is required of me and sure too that this it is only in the Risen Christ true security is to be found.

When I started to write these letters I expected to continue to write till I could write no more. The letters have been the means by which I have reflected upon my own journey and in sharing these reflections I hope that in some small way they have been of help and interest to others. However, the time of reflecting and understanding has now passed, it is now a time of "abandonment" to what is, and so this will be my final letter. All that is now required of me is to give myself to the Process of New Life that already has me firmly in its grip. I do not know and do not care how long my life expectancy is; all I aspire to is to simply live my dying with as much faith and courage as I can muster.

Initially I was very much against the publication of the letters you have received but once again I have changed my mind! I don't want them published commercially but I am happy to have my Order publish them as part of its St. Peregrine ministry to those afflicted by cancer. I have written a Forward to the letters and my Provincial and good friend, Fr. Patrick Ryall, has agreed to include in the book what will by my funeral homily. In due course the little book will be obtainable from:

The Servite Priory, Benburb, Dungannon, Co. Tyrone, N. Ireland. BT71 7JZ.

I have ensured that you will receive news of my death as and when the time comes via e-mail and would ask you to circulate that information as and how you deem appropriate.

Many thanks for your accompaniment over the past two and a half years. Keep me in your heart as I shall always keep you in mine for by so doing we will bring each other to that fullness of life promised in the Gospel. We human beings are capable of infinite expansion.

Homily given by Fr Patrick M. Ryall OSM, Prior Provincial, at the Funeral Mass for Bro. Peter Broadhurst OSM
Monday 11 June 2007

My Brothers and Sisters, the death of a beloved Brother leaves us all emotionally drained, facing a deep sense of loss and absence, yet grateful for what has been lived. Without a Good Friday there can be no Easter Sunday. When I got back from Dundee to my room on the night of Thursday, 31st May, the day after Peter died, I turned on my telephone answering machine to discover the first message on it was from Peter. He had phoned me the Friday before to inform me that he was going into hospital to die. He made one or two sarcastic remarks about my message on the answering service - why change a life-time habit! But he then shared a reflection with me referring to a discussion we had on Iona nearly three years ago. His voice was weak. The Scriptures, he said, come alive when we read them as a commentary on our own lives. They are really full of life when we see our lives in the Scripture.

As you know Peter left nothing to chance. He not only prepared spiritually for his death, but he also prepared the practical details of his funeral Mass. He chose the Readings and hymns for today's Mass, and left me clear instructions to concentrate on the Resurrection in the homily and not to deliver a panegyric!! To the best of my ability I will do as instructed and let the Scriptures speak for themselves. They will speak to us of God, of his goodness, of his promise to stay with us, and of the ultimate victory of his love in our living and dying. They will speak to us of Peter, of his times of joy and his times of suffering, of his moments of loneliness and his moments of companionship. He journeyed in the sure knowledge that the Risen Lord walked with him. Jesus is so close to us that his story and our stories merge. Christ's story, glory achieved through suffering and death - helps us to make sense of our own story and throws light on it, and points us in the direction of our destiny with God. In the second Reading St Paul tells us: " With God on our side who can be against us? When God acquits, could anyone condemn? Could Christ Jesus? No! He not only died for us, he rose from the dead, and there at God's right hand he stands and pleads for us. " St Paul goes on to explain the Christian conviction: "For I am certain of this, neither death nor life, no angel, no prince, nothing that exists, nothing still to come, not any power, or height or depth, nor any created thing, can ever come between us and the love of God made visible in Christ Jesus our lord". [Roms. 8..3 7-39].

Those powerful words of St Paul capture the faith conviction that characterised the disciples of Jesus after his death and Resurrection. It gradually dawned on them that Jesus, whom they loved and looked up to, was not held in the grasp of death; death had not annihilated him. He was alive - still with them, present to them. They put it in real graphic language - "We ate and drank with him, we touched him". Their Lord, Jesus Christ, was not restricted or confined by death. He was alive, active in their midst and influencing their lives. Jesus had gone through a process of dying, the power of God's love had taken him through the experience and raised him up, beyond its grasp and grip, Christ is Risen.

This is the faith of the Christian Church. Those of us who knew Peter, in whatever capacity, know too that this was the faith which Peter lived. It was this faith-vision enabled him to live life to the full. It was this faith that empowered him to accept the reality of the terminal cancer when it was diagnosed, and helped him adjust to, the impending consequences and limitations imposed on him by the devastating effects of mesothelioma. He was aware too that he would need the best medical care and expertise available, together with the love and support of family and friends. In the secure embrace of all these elements he could live and he could die; and all those gifts were there in abundance when he most needed them.

To believe in Christ's Resurrection stretches and expands our secular mind-set. Resurrection enables us to cross the frontier between time and eternity and between life and death. As St John put it in the Gospel passage chosen by Peter for today's Mass, "Yes, it is my father's will that whoever sees the Son and believes in him shall have eternal life, and that I shall raise him up on the last day." Peter had seen the Son and tasted eternal life. All those united to Christ through faith share that vision and awareness and see dying and rising as a process of entering more fully into life. Each day brings its own awareness of loss, of letting go, of surrender to what is, but also the dawning awareness of gain, of further growth, of deeper enrichment within. This process can, and indeed is very painful, causing much suffering and even resistance within us. Hence, there is always the temptation to avoid the challenge, to escape and be carried away by whatever distraction presents itself. If you take the escape route you die before your time, and you put off an encounter with Resurrection. In one of his reflections Peter wrote, "Dying and rising are built into the very structure of creation; things come into being then pass away, and we are no exception to this process".

We may try to resist it, avoid it or escape it kicking and screaming, but if growth is to happen and true life is to emerge then the ego has to surrender and die each day so that the true self, the redeemed self can grow and mature and come to life. That is the daily journey towards fulfillment. As Peter put it: "Dying is the price to be paid for enhancement at each and every stage of life; it is a dying in order to live ". Quoting St John of the Cross: "He who knows how to die in all things will have life in all things ".

This process of coming to new life, we believe, God has shown us in Jesus Christ. In the life, death and Resurrection of Jesus Christ we see the transforming power of God's love at work. His Resurrection gives us sure hope, inviting us to look to a future. To a beyond, to an ever expanding of time into eternity. We get a glimpse of the spaciousness of the Kingdom and the utter vastness of God. This is what you get when you are "in Christ". When attached to Christ by faith, the natural limits and boundaries are transcended. In the Resurrection of Jesus Christ we celebrate God's liberating love for his beloved Son, and his liberating love for all who follow the way of the beloved Son.

This was the faith vision that inspired Peter throughout his life. He expressed it throughout his different ministries. The call to live more fully was practiced in his Nursing and especially his psychotherapy work. Helping people to grow in self understanding he invited them to re-shape their broken lives and begin a process of healing leading to wholeness. Through his compassionate yet challenging presence he put people in touch with what needed to die and what needed to live in their lives.

This inner journey was further nourished through the practice of Christian Meditation, with the help of centering prayer we touch the deep centre within where the Divine in us dwells - here we meet the indwelling God, who invites us to let go of superficiality and to surrender to the Presence. Peter wholeheartedly embraced the solitary lifestyle so that contemplative prayer could be the dominant feature of his Christian and Servite life. He broke the Word of God for so many through his ministry as a guide to numerous Christian Meditation Groups. His ministry in this area touched and changed so many and for some triggered off a Resurrection experience in their relationship with God. With the eyes of faith he had glimpsed the Son, and what he saw he wanted to share with others. Eternal life is possible for all who meet the real Christ.

As a Servite, he revisited Servite Marian Spirituality. His favourite Marian Icon was that of the Pregnant Virgin. Here was flesh and blood, suffering and coming to birth. All of us have the potential to give birth to the Divine life within us, and to let the Word become flesh in our lives. His cancer forced him to look again at St Peregrine and the ministry of christian healing. His reflections culminated in the booklet: St Peregrine - An alternative Viewpoint. For him regular contact with Christ was maintained through the Scriptures, contemplative prayer and the Eucharist. The Eucharist is the means by which we are sacramentally united to the Dying and Rising Christ.

Some years ago at a Provincial meeting, we were invited by our facilitator to put our mission for today into words. Many of us wrote sentences, some even paragraphs, yet Peter simply wrote "Be Christ today". This is surely what we are all called to, whatever our vocation in life may be. We are called to incarnate the Word of the living God - life's task for all of us, so now "Be Christ today". We give thanks for Peter's life, for his friendship, companionship, his brotherliness, his sense of humour, his directness and no nonsense attitude. We all benefitted from knowing him. He never stopped giving - even in his last months he allowed himself to be interviewed by some medical students at the behest of Professor Rankine so that they could benefit from his cancer experience. It was a deeply moving and productive experience for all involved. We give thanks for Peter's Religious Life - for his faith expressed in, meditation Prayer. By his faith he challenged us to be authentic. Peter taught us how to live well and how to die well, so we give back his life in gratitude to God. Peter knew he was loved, he knew he belonged and was valued by so many. His courageous coming to terms with his own dying, inspired many and challenged us all.

Close to him in his final days and hours, Marie, myself and Margaret read to him the chapters of St John's Gospel which he had requested, and so in the medical love and care of ward 32 of Ninewells Hospital we had the sense that it was the time to transfer him from the safe human hands he trusted so much to the safe and loving hands of the Almighty Father. We entrusted him to the secure and loving hands of God the hands that guide us through life's complex journey. With faith and trust in God we are enlightened and comforted by those words of our first Reading from the Book of Wisdom: "The souls of the virtuous in the hands of God, no torment shall ever touch them their going looked like a disaster, their leaving us, like annihilation, but they are in peace." In that embrace we leave our Brother, Peter. Thank you, Peter, and enjoy that Peace.